SALT & LIGHT

A STUDY *of* BIBLICAL METAPHORS *for the* CHRISTIAN LIFE

MARK RASMUSSEN

First published in 2010 by Striving Together Publications, a ministry of Lancaster Baptist Church, Lancaster, CA 93535. Striving Together Publications is committed to providing tried, trusted, and proven books that will further equip local churches to carry out the Great Commission. Your comments and suggestions are valued.

Striving Together Publications
4020 E. Lancaster Blvd.
Lancaster, CA 93535
800.201.7748

Cover design by Andrew Jones
Layout by Craig Parker
Edited by Monica Bass
Special thanks to our proofreaders.

ISBN 978–1–59894–095–4

Printed in the United States of America

Table of Contents

How to Use This Curriculum

Take a moment to familiarize yourself with the features of this *Striving Together* Sunday school curriculum:

Schedule

The lessons contained in this curriculum are undated, allowing you to begin and end the teaching series at any time. There are thirteen lessons that may be taught weekly any time of the year.

Student Edition Books

Companion books are available through *Striving Together Publications*. These contain:

- The outlines with blanks that students may fill in during the lessons

- Various Scripture quotations that are used throughout each lesson
- The introductory lesson overviews
- Study questions for review throughout the week
- A suggested memory verse for each lesson

These books are excellent tools for the members of a class. We suggest ordering enough books for each member of the class, plus additional copies for new members who enroll in the class throughout the teaching series. Giving class members a study book encourages faithfulness to the class, provides students with a devotional tool for use throughout the week, and allows them to review what they learned previously.

Text

The verses from which the lessons are taken are included at the beginning of each lesson. These are provided so that you may read them through several times in prayerful preparation for your time in class. Many teachers choose to memorize their key verses. During the class hour, we suggest that you use your own Bible for Scripture reading and encourage your class members to do so as well.

Overview and Lesson Theme

The overview and theme sections are provided so that you may be aware of the overall emphasis of each lesson, especially as they relate to the other lessons in the curriculum. These brief statements provide a snapshot of where each lesson will take the students.

Lesson Goals

Bible teaching has a higher goal than the delivery of information. That goal is a life changed. Students want to know what they are to do with what they are given from God's Word. As you prepare for and teach each lesson, emphasize how those listening may apply its truths throughout the week.

Teaching Outline

The abbreviated outline enables you to view the entire lesson at a glance to see how the content fits together. Teaching with an organized outline increases the students' abilities to understand and remember the lesson content.

LESSON ONE

Salt and Light in Our World

Text

MATTHEW 5:13–16

13 *Ye are the salt of the earth: but if the salt have lost his savour,*
wherewith shall it be salted? it is thenceforth good for nothing,
but to be cast out, and to be trodden under foot of men.
14 *Ye are the light of the world. A city that is set on an hill*
cannot be hid.
15 *Neither do men light a candle, and put it under a bushel,*
but on a candlestick; and it giveth light unto all that are in
the house.
16 *Let your light so shine before men, that they may see your*
good works, and glorify your Father which is in heaven.

Overview

Jesus used two simple objects to illustrate our role as Christians—salt and light. Both have unique qualities and fulfill important functions that should be demonstrated by Christians in the world today.

Lesson Theme

God has given us the privilege of representing Him. By understanding the basic functions of salt and light and by applying their attributes to our daily lives, we will be able to fulfill God's purpose for our lives and to bring others to the Lord.

Lesson Goals

At the conclusion of the lesson, each student should:

1. Know the basic purposes of salt and light.
2. Understand how salt and light relate to the Christian's responsibility to bring others to the Lord.
3. Choose to be a savory Christian who walks close enough to the Lord to reflect His light.

Teaching Outline

Introduction

I. Salt
   A. Salt preserves.
   B. Salt purifies.
   C. Salt pleases.
   D. Salt prods.

II. Light
   A. Light attracts.
   B. Light repels.
   C. Light requires a source.
      1. God is light.
      2. The Bible is light.

Conclusion

LESSON ONE

Salt and Light in Our World

Text

MATTHEW 5:13–16

13 *Ye are the salt of the earth: but if the salt have lost his savour, wherewith shall it be salted? it is thenceforth good for nothing, but to be cast out, and to be trodden under foot of men.*

14 *Ye are the light of the world. A city that is set on an hill cannot be hid.*

15 *Neither do men light a candle, and put it under a bushel, but on a candlestick; and it giveth light unto all that are in the house.*

16 *Let your light so shine before men, that they may see your good works, and glorify your Father which is in heaven.*

Introduction

Our Lord often used common illustrations to teach great truths. In Matthew 5:13–16, He tells His people that they are the "*salt of the earth*" and the "*light of the world.*"

Salt and light both work a beneficial change—they make a positive difference! God desires to use us to make a positive difference—to have a real and lasting impact for His glory.

For a beneficial change to occur, the salt must not remain in the shaker, and the light must not be hidden. Likewise, the qualities of light and salt in the lives of Christians should be manifested, not hidden or diluted. God wants us to make a difference in this world as Jesus did. The Bible says in Acts 10:38 that Jesus *"went about doing good,"* and 1 Peter 2:21 reminds us that we are to *"follow his steps."* First John 4:17 tells us that *"as he is, so are we in this world."*

As we study the qualities of salt and light, we can better understand the ways God commands us to make a difference in the lives of others.

I. Salt

Every cook needs some basic spices to produce a desirable meal. While there are hundreds of different spices, salt is the one spice that just about every cook uses consistently. In Matthew 5, our Lord used salt to illustrate the effect His people should have in this world. As we examine its qualities, we can gain more understanding of His words, "*Ye are the salt of the earth*" (Matthew 5:13).

A. Salt preserves.

The goal of preservation is twofold: to seal the good and to shut out the impurities or decay. Salt, as a preserving agent, keeps food from spoilage. If you open a jar of homemade strawberry jam, you do not expect to see a layer of mold or fungus settled on top, because the seal protects the jam from that which might cause corruption.

Today, with refrigerators and freezers, as well as food loaded with preservatives, we don't clearly understand the use of salt as a preservative. In Bible days, however, salt was a necessary and frequently used preservative.

Nehemiah 13:16 records the story of the men of Tyre who brought their fish to sell in Jerusalem. The distance from Tyre to Jerusalem, as a crow flies, is almost one hundred miles. Would you like to carry a load of dead fish one hundred miles under the hot sun of the Middle East and then try to sell it? How did they keep it from spoiling? The men of Tyre used salt from the Mediterranean Sea to preserve the fish until they could sell it in Jerusalem.

In the early days of America, the settlers used salt to preserve meat. They didn't have grocery stores and meat markets. If they wanted meat, they had to go out and shoot it. Once they killed the animal and dressed it (or "gutted" it, to put it a little less delicately), they would rub it thoroughly with salt and hang it over a fire in their smokehouse to dry. This process would preserve the meat and allow them to keep it for months.

As Christians, God wants us to act as an agent of preservation in this world. We live in an evil and corrupt world today, yet I believe God is mercifully withholding His final judgment because there are still some people who love Him and desire to make a difference for Him. For example, in spite of the rampant wickedness of Sodom and Gomorrah, ten righteous people could have preserved those cities from the wrath of God (Genesis 18:32). Let's live righteously before God and help others to be right with God so that there can be more salt in this world.

Illustration

In Roman times, salt was so important for preserving food that soldiers were sometimes paid in salt. From this came the phrase, "a man who is worth his salt."

The salty Christian will help to protect himself, his family, and his church from the damaging influences of the world. Salt will help to thwart the entrance of sin or compromise that brings about an undesirable change in the life of the believer or his family.

Many passages command us to guard against the damage of sin. Jesus instructed, "*Have salt in yourselves*" (Mark 9:50). The characteristic of "salt" in our lives will preserve us, keeping us from sin and a life that displeases God.

James 1:27
27 *Pure religion and undefiled before God and the Father is this, …to keep himself unspotted from the world.*

Proverbs 4:23
23 *Keep thy heart with all diligence; for out of it are the issues of life.*

Psalm 34:13
13 *Keep thy tongue from evil, and thy lips from speaking guile.*

1 Timothy 6:20
20 *…keep that which is committed to thy trust…*

1 Timothy 5:22
22 *…neither be partaker of other men's sins: keep thyself pure.*

1 John 5:21

21 *Little children, keep yourselves from idols…*

B. Salt purifies.

Illustration

A friend once told me about a huge head of broccoli about the size of a soccer ball he cut from his garden. Upon the instructions of his wife, he immersed it in a solution of salt water. Over an hour later he took the broccoli out of the salt water and rinsed it thoroughly. He was quite surprised to see that about a dozen green worms of various sizes and various stages of death had come out of the broccoli. Salt purifies!

Illustration

Salt water purifies by killing germs. This is why gargling with warm salt water often brings relief to a sore throat.

No matter where we are or what we are doing, God expects us to have a purifying influence. The spiritual environment ought to be cleaner and more wholesome because we are there. What kind of influence do you have on those around you? Are people directed toward God by your presence, or are they dragged down? When you walk into a room, does it gain a godlier atmosphere, or does the spiritual temperature drop?

As Christians, we are purified through time spent with God in His Word. The Bible gives several illustrations of those who have fulfilled the purifying role of salt because of their time in God's presence. Exodus 34:29–35 tells how the face of Moses glowed when he descended from Mount Sinai after being in the presence of God. He was unaware of this glow until the people told him. Moses was different in a way that he did not even realize because he had spent intense personal time with God Himself.

Peter and John were changed men because of their intimacy with the Lord. "*Now when they saw the boldness of Peter and John, and perceived that they were unlearned and ignorant men, they marvelled; and they took knowledge of them, that they had been with Jesus*" (Acts 4:13). Can others tell that you have been with Jesus?

In the Philippian jail, "*Paul and Silas prayed, and sang praises unto God: and the prisoners heard them*" (Acts 16:25). Jail can be a gloomy and fearful place (so I've heard—I've never experienced it!), and yet the presence of God in the lives of His people completely transformed the atmosphere. When God sent the earthquake, instead of escaping, all of the other prisoners stayed to hear the Word of God. The jailer himself believed on the Lord Jesus Christ and was saved. Even as Paul and Silas were suffering physically, they were a purifying influence in jail.

Do you have a purifying, cleansing influence in your daily life? You cannot have a positive, spiritual influence on others if your life is not clean. It is hard to take that which is dirty and use it to make something clean! When you wash dishes, do you start with dirty water? When you wash your car, do you start with dirty sponges? Of course not! And so God, as He desires for us to have a purifying and cleansing influence on the world, needs our lives to be pure and clean.

Living a clean life will occur only if we choose to do so. This choice is not easy in a filthy, corrupt world, but it is necessary.

In Titus 2:14, we read that our Lord "*gave himself for us, that he might redeem us from all iniquity, and purify unto himself a peculiar people, zealous of good works.*" People who desire to live clean lives and refuse to participate in this world's sinful pleasures, are indeed considered peculiar! James 4:8 reminds us, "*Draw nigh to God, and he will draw nigh to you. Cleanse your hands, ye sinners; and purify your hearts, ye double minded.*"

Proverbs 4:23 says, "*Keep thy heart with all diligence; for out of it are the issues of life.*" What comes out in your life is a direct result of what is in your heart. Are you careful to feed your heart and mind with clean and godly influences so God can use your life to be a purifying and cleansing influence on those around you?

Illustration

During the Civil War, the medical staff of the Confederate armies often found themselves without the necessary medical and pharmaceutical resources they needed. They were forced to resort to rudimentary medical treatments in their attempts to save the lives of wounded soldiers. Gangrene was a constant threat for a soldier who had been shot. The medics found, however, that if they could immediately get salt into the wound, the gangrene might be prevented. Some surgeons would pull a piece of cloth saturated with salt through the wound in an attempt to retard potential infection.

During the great days of the English Navy, sailors who had been flogged for disobedience would have salt rubbed into their open wounds to clean the wounds and speed the healing process. Sometimes they would actually be tied to a rope and pushed overboard into the sea, so the salt water would get into the wounds. If the seas were too rough for this, they might be lowered headfirst into a barrel of brine instead.

Although one goal of this process was healing so the flogged sailors could get back to work as quickly as possible, it seems likely that the agony of the salt treatment also served as a further deterrent to future disobedience. So salt purified the wounds as well as the behavior!

C. Salt pleases.

Without salt, foods would be bland.

Job 6:6

6 *Can that which is unsavoury be eaten without salt? or is there any taste in the white of an egg?*

Illustration

While attending Bible college, I worked as a cook for a family restaurant in St. John, Indiana, called Traveler's Restaurant. As I was learning my new job, I was more of a cook's helper than an actual line cook. A chef would come in the morning and do the major cooking of the sauces and soups and main entrées for the day. I still remember two of these chefs, Eddie and Jack. On a shelf right above the stove was a container that held a mixture of salt and small amounts of pepper and garlic. It seemed as though pinches or dashes of this mixture were used in virtually everything Eddie and Jack made. I soon learned that the addition of these spices created a pungency that pleased the palate.

Illustration

Most people keep their salt shakers handy as they eat, and they don't hesitate to sprinkle it freely on their foods.

Many even add salt to fries from McDonald's or In-N-Out Burger (a favorite southern California burger chain), even though they are already heavily salted.

God's people are also to please. We can be a great encouragement to others by using our words appropriately, saying the right thing at the right time. This can be a sad and difficult world. When people need a smile and a kind word, can they count on you for it? I have often been encouraged by the words of other people, and I want God to use me in the same way.

Proverbs 25:11
11 *A word fitly spoken is like apples of gold in pictures of silver.*

Proverbs 15:23
23 *A man hath joy by the answer of his mouth: and a word spoken in due season, how good is it!*

Isaiah 50:4
4 *The Lord God hath given me the tongue of the learned, that I should know how to speak a word in season to him that is weary…*

We have all heard the statement "sticks and stones may break my bones, but words can never hurt me." But we all know from personal experience how false this statement is. Words are powerful; words can hurt.

Illustration

Adolph Hitler led the German people down a path of destruction during the 1930s and into World War II. He brought untold misery to many millions, primarily through the power of his words. On the other hand, Winston Churchill used his words to inspire the British people to maintain their hope and fight the Nazi menace during the dark days of 1940 when Britain stood alone and all seemed hopeless.

The words that come out of our mouths are flavored by the condition of our hearts.

Matthew 12:34

34 ...out of the abundance of the heart the mouth speaketh.

If our hearts are what they ought to be, we will say what we ought to say. When our heart is right, God can use our words to be an encouragement and a means of helping others grow.

Proverbs 16:21–24

21 *The wise in heart shall be called prudent: and the sweetness of the lips increaseth learning.*
22 *Understanding is a wellspring of life unto him that hath it: but the instruction of fools is folly.*
23 *The heart of the wise teacheth his mouth, and addeth learning to his lips.*
24 *Pleasant words are as an honeycomb, sweet to the soul, and health to the bones.*

D. Salt prods.

We've all heard, "You can lead a horse to water, but you can't make him drink." This is only partially true. You can't make a horse drink, but you can make him want to drink by giving him salt.

Illustration

Farmers with livestock provide salt blocks (as big as twenty-five or fifty pounds) for their animals. The livestock have a natural craving for the salt, and it creates a thirst as well.

Illustration

The early American settlers made good use of salt in their hunting. Instead of walking through the woods hoping to see a deer, they often hid themselves near a "salt lick." This was a natural deposit of exposed salt they knew would attract deer. As the deer came to lick the salt, the hunter could get an easy shot.

As God's people, our "saltiness" for God attracts others to Him. If we have a peace, joy, and strength that carries us through all circumstances, others will want what we have. God uses us to create a thirst in them, so they too can know the One who gives them the living water so that they never thirst again.

John 4:13–14

13 *Jesus answered and said unto her, Whosoever drinketh of this water shall thirst again:*

14 *But whosoever drinketh of the water that I shall give him shall never thirst; but the water that I shall give him shall be in him a well of water springing up into everlasting life.*

II. Light

Not only are we the *"salt of the earth;"* we are also the *"light of the world."* God has placed us in a dark world, and we are to reflect the light of Jesus, who is the light of the world.

John 8:12

12 *Then spake Jesus again unto them, saying, I am the light of the world: he that followeth me shall not walk in darkness, but shall have the light of life.*

The intensity of the darkness around us makes great our responsibility to be the bearers and keepers of God's light.

A. Light attracts.

Light is one of the most attractive forces on earth.

Illustration

Next time you go to a nighttime ballgame, look up at the giant bank of lights illuminating the field. You will see untold multitudes of insects all getting to watch the game for free! They were attracted by the lights from miles around.

Years ago, the preacher John Wesley, whose light attracted many others, summed up his ministry like this: "I light myself on fire, and people come to watch me burn." Great men like Wesley, Whitefield, Edwards, and others have truly been lights for God.

God tells us to make our lights visible.

Matthew 5:16

16 *Let your light so shine before men, that they may see your good works, and glorify your Father which is in heaven.*

Some think that the lifestyle of a monk or a nun, shut away from the world, is the way to truly live for God.

Illustration

Church history tells us of a group of men called the Anchorites who lived in the fourth century. They dwelt in solitude, fasted, and injured their bodies. The nearer they could bring themselves to the level of the animals the better pleased they were. One sect of Anchorites actually grazed with the common herds in the fields of Mesopotamia, and they were hence called *boskoi*, or *shepherds.* They acquired a great reputation for holiness because of their mournful attitude toward life.

One of the most famous of these monks was Simeon Stylites (AD 395–451), so called from his standing for years on the top of a column sixty feet high until his muscles became rigid. Some of these hermits hung weights on their bodies; others kept themselves in cages; all endeavored to make themselves holy through being miserable.

The motive of these men may have been truly honorable, a desire to escape from the vices of the great cities. But the greater the corruption of society, the more need for holy men and women to live in that society. The world can only become darker by the withdrawing of its lights and more corrupt through the removing of the salt scattered over it. [Source: 2000+ Bible Illustrations]

The Word of God, however, tells us to be in the world but not of the world.

Philippians 2:14–16

14 *Do all things without murmurings and disputings:*

15 *That ye may be blameless and harmless, the sons of*
God, without rebuke, in the midst of a crooked and perverse
nation, among whom ye shine as lights in the world;
16 *Holding forth the word of life; that I may rejoice in the*
day of Christ, that I have not run in vain, neither laboured
in vain.

1 John 2:15–17

15 *Love not the world, neither the things that are in the*
world. If any man love the world, the love of the Father is
not in him.
16 *For all that is in the world, the lust of the flesh, and the*
lust of the eyes, and the pride of life, is not of the Father,
but is of the world.
17 *And the world passeth away, and the lust thereof: but*
he that doeth the will of God abideth for ever.

God has left us here to be a reflection of His light to a very dark world. Jesus said of John the Baptist, "*He was a burning and a shining light*" (John 5:35). Many came to know God through the ministry of John the Baptist. We are to be lights as well, attracting people to the Lord.

Matthew 5:16

16 *Let your light so shine before men, that they may see your good works, and glorify your Father which is in heaven.*

John 3:21

21 *But he that doeth truth cometh to the light, that his deeds may be made manifest, that they are wrought in God.*

We could ask ourselves the question, "Do people see Jesus in me?"

B. Light repels.

Light attracts, but light also repels the darkness.

Illustration

If you have ever taken a tour of a cavern or a cave where the lights were turned out, you have experienced total darkness. You literally cannot see your hand in front of your face. In this kind of darkness, one small light can make a real difference.

Illustration

Before the days of electric lights in Victorian England, the streets were lined with gas lamps. Men called "lamplighters" had the job of going down the street and poking a lighted torch into the gas lamps, creating a warm glow that would dissipate the darkness. Charles Spurgeon of London observed these lamplighters and said that we Christians are to be lamplighters for God, poking holes in the darkness of this world.

God has commanded us to make a difference in the environment in which He has placed us. The song titled "Jesus Bids Us Shine" conveys the importance of this truth.

> Jesus bids us shine
> With a pure, clear light,
> Like a little candle
> Burning in the night.
> In this world of darkness
> We must shine—
> You in your small corner,
> And I in mine.

Illustration

One of my college roommates, Rich, told me about the rats that ran rampant in the restaurant where he worked. His story seemed beyond the bounds of reality to me, so one night he offered to show me the rats. Because I grew up in southern California and had never seen a rat running around our home, I thought this would be a great adventure. Rich unlocked the back door of the restaurant and threw a piece of cold, fried chicken into the corner of a stairwell. He then turned off the lights and waited a few moments. When he turned on the lights, I almost screamed in horror as I saw the rats scurrying for the cover of darkness! Even though that was almost three decades ago, my skin almost crawls with the thought of those vile creatures coming out of the darkness where they hid.

Illustration

It is interesting to note, as one drives down the street and looks into a bar or a saloon, how dark they often are. Even today, men still love darkness rather than light (John 3:19).

Christ's light has the power to repel darkness, and He has given us the responsibility to reflect His light.

C. Light requires a source.

If we are to reflect the light of the Lord, we must understand the Source of this light. Where does it come from? God Himself is our source of light.

JAMES 1:17

17 *Every good gift and every perfect gift is from above, and cometh down from the Father of lights, with whom is no variableness, neither shadow of turning.*

1 JOHN 1:5

5 *This then is the message which we have heard of him, and declare unto you, that God is light, and in him is no darkness at all.*

When we walk with God, we have all the light we need.

PSALM 27:1

1 *The LORD is my light and my salvation; whom shall I fear? the LORD is the strength of my life; of whom shall I be afraid?*

PSALM 36: 9

9 *...in thy light shall we see light.*

1 JOHN 1:7

7 *But if we walk in the light, as he is in the light, we have fellowship one with another, and the blood of Jesus Christ his Son cleanseth us from all sin.*

Acts 9 tells of Saul's conversion on the road to Damascus. The light that shined on him was so strong that he was stricken blind. This was the light of the Lord's presence.

ACTS 26:13

13 *At midday, O king, I saw in the way a light from heaven, above the brightness of the sun, shining round about me and them which journeyed with me.*

When we walk with the Lord, some people will be drawn to the light we reflect while some will hate it. Light always has the quality of being pleasurable to some and irritating to others.

The closer we are to our Heavenly Father, the more we will be like Him.

Illustration

There have been many Christians of yesteryear—some famous, and many more unknown—who have allowed God to work in such a personal and powerful way in them that wherever they went, they radiated God's light. It was said of one circuit-riding preacher that he was a traveling lighthouse. The Holy Spirit used him to fuel a flame of righteousness for God.

We must live in such a way that God is so real and personal to us that others will see His light reflected from our lives, even as the moon reflects the light of the sun.

Another source of light for the Christian is God's Word. If the Word of God is truly part of us, it will shine through us.

The longest chapter in the Bible, Psalm 119, focuses on the Word of God.

PSALM 119:105

105 Thy word is a lamp unto my feet, and a light unto my path.

PSALM 119:130

130 The entrance of thy words giveth light; it giveth understanding unto the simple.

Peter wrote of the Word of God as a "*light that shineth in a dark place*" (2 Peter 1:19). It is the light of the Scripture that shows us what we need to work on and change in our lives. The light of the Word of God reveals the darkness of our sin and illumines the presence of God.

It is vital, then, that we read, memorize, and meditate on the Word of God so that the light of God can effectively shine both on us and through us.

Illustration

Around the year 1450, Johannes Gutenberg of Germany built the first printing press in the Western world. Gutenberg is most famous for the Gutenberg Bible, which today is one of the most valuable books ever printed. With the invention of the printing press, the Bible became far more accessible and less expensive than the Scriptures which had previously been hand-copied by scribes and monks. When the Bible was finally translated from the ancient languages into the languages of the common people, it was widely distributed. The translation and distribution of God's Word were the key factors in bringing about the Reformation. The spreading of the light of the Word of God brought about the end of the "Dark Ages."

Conclusion

The key aspect of both salt and light is that they make a difference in their surroundings. When our lives fulfill the basic functions of salt and light, we, too, will make a difference in the lives of others for the cause of Christ.

God has given us the privilege and responsibility of representing Him. Let's allow God's Word to make a difference in us, so we can make a difference for God.

Study Questions

1. What are some of the basic purposes of salt?
   Salt preserves, purifies, pleases, and prods.

2. How can a horse be prodded to drink water? And how does this relate to our role as salt?
   A horse that is given salt will want water. When Christians display the peace and joy of the Lord during times of trouble, others will be drawn to their Source of strength.

3. What are the two sources of a Christian's light?
   God and the Bible are our sources of light.

4. Will everyone's response to the light be positive?
   No, some people are attracted to light, and others are repelled by it.

5. Who is in your circle of influence that needs you to be a "salty" Christian who reflects God's light?
   Answers will vary but could include the following: unsaved family members, neighbors, co-workers, discouraged church members, children, etc.

6. Using the basic functions of salt as described in this lesson as indicators, on a scale of one to ten, how salty of a Christian are you?
   Answers will vary.

7. What are some steps of action you can take to fulfill the basic purposes of salt this week?
   Answers will vary but could include the following: guard myself and my family against worldliness, feed my mind with pure influences, look for ways to encourage others, etc.

8. Are you faithfully reading, memorizing, and meditating on God's Word? How can you incorporate these disciplines into your daily life?
   Answers will vary but could include the following: I could rise earlier in the morning (which may include going to bed earlier with clothes laid out for the next day) to spend time with the Lord, or I need to create a Scripture memory schedule, or I need to find an accountability partner to keep me on track.

Memory Verse

Matthew 5:13–14

13 *Ye are the salt of the earth: but if the salt have lost his savour,*
wherewith shall it be salted? it is thenceforth good for nothing,
but to be cast out, and to be trodden under foot of men.
14 *Ye are the light of the world. A city that is set on an hill*
cannot be hid.

LESSON TWO

A Farmer in God's Harvest

Text

2 TIMOTHY 2:6

6 *The husbandman that laboureth must be first partaker of the fruits.*

Overview

A bountiful harvest is simply the visible result of a farmer's earlier duties performed faithfully. As laborers for God, we too, must work to see an abundant harvest. In this lesson, we examine some of the farmer's tasks and relate them to our responsibilities as God's husbandmen.

Lesson Theme

A farmer's job is not easy, but it is rewarding! As God's harvest field laborers, we must be willing to prepare the ground, obedient to plant the seed and prune the crops, and ultimately, diligent to possess the harvest that the Lord gives.

Lesson Objectives

At the conclusion of the lesson, each student should:

1. Examine their life for anything that would hinder a great harvest.
2. Understand the importance of faithfully spending time in God's Word for conviction and growth.

3. Be determined to be actively involved in gathering God's harvest.

Teaching Outline

Introduction

- I. The Farmer Prepares
  - A. Clearing
  - B. Plowing
- II. The Farmer Plants
  - A. Planting the seed
  - B. Pruning the crops
- III. The Farmer Possesses
  - A. The time to harvest is now.
  - B. The time of harvest brings rejoicing.

Conclusion

LESSON TWO

A Farmer in God's Harvest

Text

2 TIMOTHY 2:6

6 *The husbandman that laboureth must be first partaker of the fruits.*

Introduction

Farming is hard, laborious, and arduous work. It should not be the occupation of choice for one who is expecting recreation and relaxation. So it is with farming in God's harvest fields. It is not simple, and it is not easy; but if we are faithful, the harvest will truly be glorious.

To gain a bountiful harvest, the farmer must perform several significant tasks. The harvest is simply the visible result of those preliminary steps performed faithfully. These steps are not as noticeable as a rich harvest, but without them there would be no harvest.

Let's look at some of the tasks a farmer must perform to enjoy a worthwhile harvest.

I. The Farmer Prepares

The farmer must first prepare the soil. Luke 13:6–9 gives the story of a man who understood that preparation precedes harvest.

Luke 13:6–9

6 *He spake also this parable; A certain man had a fig tree planted in his vineyard; and he came and sought fruit thereon, and found none.*

7 *Then said he unto the dresser of his vineyard, Behold, these three years I come seeking fruit on this fig tree, and find none: cut it down; why cumbereth it the ground?*

8 *And he answering said unto him, Lord, let it alone this year also, till I shall dig about it, and dung it:*

9 *And if it bear fruit, well: and if not, then after that thou shalt cut it down.*

To give the fig tree another opportunity to bear fruit, the dresser of this vineyard promised to *"dig about it, and dung it"*—to break up the ground around the tree and fertilize it. Preparation must come before harvest.

A. Clearing

Illustration

Years ago, Pastor Chappell's family moved to the area of Cortez, Colorado, and began to clear fields for the pinto and garbanzo beans from which they would make their living. They had to remove brush, stumps, and stones before they could plow the fields. They had to level off high places; they had to fill in low places.

It would be ineffective and sometimes impossible to plant ground that has not been cleared.

God likens Himself to a vineyard owner who carefully gathered the stones out of his vineyard before he planted his vines.

Isaiah 5:2

2 *And he fenced it, and gathered out the stones thereof, and planted it with the choicest vine...*

We must prepare the soil of our hearts to receive the Word of God by removing anything that hinders God from working in our hearts and lives. Even as good, fertile, productive farmland must be kept clear of weeds, stumps, roots, and rocks, our hearts and lives must be kept clear of that which displeases God and hinders His work.

Second Kings 18 gives the account of young Hezekiah ascending to the throne of Judah. God records of his life, "*he did that which was right in the sight of the Lord.*" Hezekiah wanted God to work in his nation and in the lives of his people, so the first thing he did was to remove the places of idolatrous worship. He cut down the groves, removed the high places, and broke up the idols. God's biographical comment on his life is found in verses 5–6, "*He trusted in the Lord God of Israel; so that after him was none like him among all the kings of Judah, nor any that were before him. For he clave to the Lord, and departed not from following him....*" Hezekiah prepared his kingdom to follow the Lord by first clearing out the things that were displeasing to the Lord.

We easily recognize that clearing our lives for God's service includes removing sin. What we sometimes overlook, however, are things that may not be inherently sinful but have taken a wrong position in our lives. Hezekiah's cleansing of Judah provides a perfect illustration.

To understand all that Hezekiah did, you must know some background information. Seven hundred years before Hezekiah, during the time of Israel's wanderings in the wilderness, God sent fiery serpents to judge the people for their complaining, and many people died. God instructed Moses to make a serpent of brass and mount it on a pole for all to see. God then promised that anyone who looked at the brazen serpent would be healed and would live. (The hymn "Look and Live" is based on this account.)

As the years went by, the Israelites converted this brazen serpent into an idol, worshipping it and burning incense to it. The brazen serpent was a good thing that had come to be used in the wrong way. Hezekiah destroyed this object to keep it from ever again becoming a threat to the people's walk with the Lord.

2 Kings 18:4

4 *He...brake in pieces the brasen serpent that Moses had made: for unto those days the children of Israel did burn incense to it...*

We, too, may have idols of good things to which we have given the wrong position. Sometimes a favorite pastime or hobby or sport (whether we participate or observe) can take a wrong place in our lives and actually come between us and the Lord.

Illustration

Even a good thing can become a bad thing if it is in the wrong place. For example, we love our pets, but we don't normally let dogs, cats, parakeets, or iguanas into our church auditorium! We need to take care that the things we enjoy do not come between us and the Lord. Idols are not limited to graven images; an idol is anything that comes between us and God.

The farmer who wants an abundant harvest must first clear his ground.

B. Plowing

After clearing the ground, the farmer must plow.

Illustration

One of the most important inventions in American history was the steel plow, invented by John Deere. This steel plow became a great asset to the Midwest because it could easily cut through the dense soil of the area and helped to turn what some called a "great desert" into a breadbasket for the entire country. It was only when the soil was broken up that vast fields of wheat, barley, and corn could be grown.

Farmers understand that hard, sun-baked earth will not absorb moisture. Even a melting snow-pack will just run off and not soak in. Plowing and disking the ground allows the water to sink deeply into the soil and provide the moisture that will allow the crops to grow.

Our hearts need to be "plowed" as well.

Jeremiah 4:3

3 For thus saith the Lord to the men of Judah and Jerusalem, Break up your fallow ground, and sow not among thorns.

Hosea 10:12

12 *...break up your fallow ground: for it is time to seek the Lord...*

God's Word can break the hard ground of our hearts. Hebrews 4:12 tells us that *"the word of God is quick, and powerful, and sharper than any two–edged sword, piercing even to the dividing asunder of soul and spirit, and of the joints and marrow, and is a discerner of the thoughts and intents of the heart."* The Word of God can break open the hard heart and allow the seed of Scripture to bring forth fruit.

If the soil of our hearts remains unbroken, God will not accomplish what He desires in our lives. This is why it is vital for us to read and study God's Word and be faithful to church where we hear it preached.

TEACHING TIP

It would be surprising, and perhaps humbling, to know how many Christians do not spend time in God's Word faithfully. Those who have never developed this habit probably do not know where to begin or how to structure a daily meeting with God.

Provide a schedule or chart for your students to systematically read their Bibles. If you teach this lesson close to the beginning of the year, you could give them a chart to read through their Bible in a year. For starters, you might give a schedule to read through the New Testament, encouraging them to mark off chapters as they read them and also to set a goal for completion.

Encourage your students to take the first step toward developing this spiritual discipline by taking a moment to choose and schedule a time to daily meet with the Lord. This time should be guarded as carefully as any other important appointment.

Simply reading God's Word, however, is not enough. We must read it with an open and listening heart. Encourage your students to keep a record of how the Lord speaks to them through His Word in a notebook. This facilitates focused, purposeful reading, and it helps one remember how God has spoken to them and apply His truth to their daily lives.

II. The Farmer Plants

To have good crops, a farmer must start with good seed. A great deal of study, work, and care goes into the process of developing seed for thriving, productive crops.

We have been given the perfect, incorruptible seed of the Word of God.

1 Peter 1:23
23 Being born again, not of corruptible seed, but of incorruptible, by the word of God, which liveth and abideth for ever.

A. Planting the seed

Simply *having* the seed is not enough—the seed must be planted. In Haggai 2:19, the Lord asks, "*Is the seed yet in the barn?*" Crops cannot grow if the seed is left in the barn, so God asks His people why they have neglected to plant the seed of God's Word.

The "parable of the sower" in Luke 8:5–8 begins, *"A sower went out to sow his seed."* Planting the seed was this man's purpose; it was his job. He was not supposed to guard the seed carefully in the barn; he was not to hoard the seed to see how much he could accumulate; he was not to analyze and criticize the seed, speculating its possible harvest; he was not to admire the seed. Kept in the barn, the seed was useless. The sower was simply supposed to get the seed into the ground where it could grow.

As God's people, we have been given a responsibility to plant the seed of the Word of God. Unfortunately, some Christians get so caught up in inspecting the seed or the fruit, that they lose sight of their responsibility to plant.

We must not be hesitant about planting the precious seed with which we have been entrusted. Ecclesiastes 11:4 warns, *"He that observeth the wind shall not sow."* We are not to plant only when the circumstances are just right or when we are certain of the outcome. We are simply to do what God tells us to do and trust Him to bring the harvest. As General Stonewall Jackson said, "Duty is ours; the consequences are God's." Be faithful in sowing God's Word at every opportunity.

The Apostle Paul, probably the greatest Christian of the New Testament era, described himself as a planter.

1 Corinthians 3:6

6 ***I have planted,*** *Apollos watered; but God gave the increase.*

Notice that it was not Paul who controlled the harvest but God. Paul simply planted. All of us can be faithful to plant. Tell your family, friends, and co-workers about salvation. Invite them to come to church with you, and relate what God has done in your life. Some people will not respond to the Gospel the first time they hear it, but if the seed is never planted, they will never respond.

B. Pruning the crops

A farmer cannot just walk away from the newly planted seed. He must care for the plants as they grow.

Illustration

Once I visited a family's bean farm in Colorado during their daughter's teenage years. I remember so well the first time I shook her hand. She was thirteen or fourteen, but her hands felt like hardened leather. It was such an unusual feeling that I asked her about her hands. "I spend many, many hours every day hoeing the beans," she explained. The seed had been planted, but there was still work to do.

The weeds must be removed to allow the seed to grow properly. Weeds will strangle the seeds and young plants and rob from the soil the moisture and nutrients that they need to grow.

Weeds easily sprout in our lives—thoughts, attitudes, actions, and habits that hinder and strangle our Christian growth. Jesus warned of this when He told of the seed that *"fell among thorns; and the thorns sprung up, and choked them"* (Matthew 13:7).

Jesus further explained how the seed is choked in our lives. *"He also that received seed among the thorns is he that heareth the word; and the care of this world, and the deceitfulness of riches, choke the word, and he becometh unfruitful"* (Matthew 13:22). Are earthly cares and concerns or the pursuit of money choking out God's Word in your life?

Illustration

As a teenage boy, I worked for a gardener, Ron, who trained me in trimming hedges. I think this was due, in a large part, to my height and arm length that enabled me to reach over the top of a hedge that he could not normally reach. Ron made it clear to me that there was a form or shape he expected for every plant, and it was my job to remove anything that did not conform to the shape he had in mind.

Our Heavenly Father has a shape and a design in mind for each one of us, and we need to allow Him to prune us, removing from our lives anything that does not fit His will for us.

JOHN 15:1–3

1 *I am the true vine, and my Father is the husbandman.*
2 *Every branch in me that beareth not fruit he taketh away: and every branch that beareth fruit, he purgeth it, that it may bring forth more fruit.*
3 *Now ye are clean through the word which I have spoken unto you.*

Pruning is essential for a good harvest, and God uses His Word to purge, shape, and prune our lives as we obey Him.

III. The Farmer Possesses

The fall of the year brings many things to mind. We think of the colors of the foliage, of cornucopias filled with fruits and vegetables, of the Thanksgiving holiday and all that it means to us as Christians, and we certainly think of harvest.

Harvest time is the farmer's reward for months of preparing the soil and planting and pruning the crops. It is inconceivable that, after all this work, a farmer would stop short of gathering the harvest.

As Christians, we too must gather the harvest.

A. *The time to harvest is now.*

God's Word says the fields of this world are white, or ripe, unto harvest.

John 4:35–38

35 *Say not ye, There are yet four months, and then cometh harvest? behold, I say unto you, Lift up your eyes, and look on the fields; for they are white already to harvest.*
36 *And he that reapeth receiveth wages, and gathereth fruit unto life eternal: that both he that soweth and he that reapeth may rejoice together.*
37 *And herein is that saying true, One soweth, and another reapeth.*
38 *I sent you to reap that whereon ye bestowed no labour: other men laboured, and ye are entered into their labours.*

The disciples of Jesus looked on the physical fields surrounding them and knew it was not yet harvest time. But Jesus urged them to look on the fields of God, a world of people that desperately need to know the Lord. He urged them to realize that the harvest time is *now*.

If ripe crops are left in the field just a little too long, they will rot. Perhaps you've seen this in your own garden. (I've seen zucchini the size of a large torpedo!) If the harvest is not gathered at the proper time, it will soon be worthless.

Farmers clearly understand the urgency of the harvest, and they work day and night to bring the crops in at the proper time. We need to ask the Lord to give us a sense of urgency for the ripe harvest fields of souls.

B. The time of harvest brings rejoicing.

A completed harvest makes for a time of rejoicing and celebration. It brings a warm, satisfying feeling of accomplishment.

Proverbs 13:19

19 *The desire accomplished is sweet to the soul…*

Illustration

The first Thanksgiving was a special celebration held by the Pilgrims of the Plymouth colony to express their gratitude to God for the recent harvest and for all of His goodness.

Unfortunately, in today's culture, people want the celebrating *before* the harvesting. In God's divine order, however, work precedes rejoicing. In the end, all the toil invested in God's work will pale in comparison to the reward.

1 Corinthians 15:58

58 *Therefore, my beloved brethren, be ye stedfast, unmoveable, always abounding in the work of the Lord, forasmuch as ye know that your labour is not in vain in the Lord.*

Galatians 6:9

9 *And let us not be weary in well doing:* ***for in due season we shall reap, if we faint not.***

If we faithfully sow, we will experience the joy of reaping. As 1 Corinthians 3:6 explains, it is God who gives the increase, but He has chosen to use us to gather it. What a privilege!

Conclusion

As farmers and laborers in God's harvest fields, we must be willing to prepare the ground, obedient to plant the seed and prune the crops, and ultimately, diligent to possess the harvest that the Lord gives.

Study Questions

1. Why does the farmer need to prepare the ground by clearing and plowing it before planting?
   It would be ineffective, and sometimes impossible to plant ground that has not been cleared. Plowing the ground allows water to sink deeply into the soil, providing the moisture that will allow the crops to grow.

2. Why did Hezekiah destroy the brazen serpent God had previously commanded Moses to make? What does this serpent represent in our lives?
   Hezekiah destroyed the brazen serpent because the Israelites had begun to worship it. Worshipping this serpent represents anything in our lives, even good things, which have taken the wrong position.

3. What would happen if a farmer simply walked away from the fields after planting and didn't return until harvest?
   When he returned, he would find that weeds had choked his plants, and he would have a small harvest or no harvest at all.

4. Why is the harvest season urgent?
   The harvest season is urgent because the fruit will spoil and be wasted if left in the field.

5. When was the last time God spoke to you through His Word to reveal sin that needed to be removed from your life? Are you faithful to daily spend time in God's Word?
   Answers will vary.

6. Is planting the seed of God's Word by sharing the Gospel with others a regular part of your life? If not, what adjustments do you need to make to your schedule to make this a priority?
   Answers will vary.

7. Who is God laying on your heart that you could share the Gospel with this week? (Note: share these names with each other, and pray for these people throughout the week. Next week ask each other how the Lord worked.)
   Answers will vary.

8. Of the three jobs of a farmer we looked at in this lesson—preparing, planting, and possessing—where do you need to start?
   Answers will vary.

Memory Verse

2 Timothy 2:6

6 *The husbandman that laboureth must be first partaker of the fruits.*

LESSON THREE

A Student of God's Word

Text

2 TIMOTHY 2:15

15 *Study to shew thyself approved unto God, a workman that needeth not to be ashamed, rightly dividing the word of truth.*

Overview

Our typical idea of a student is "one who goes to school," but learning should not stop with graduation. We all should continue to be students our entire lives. God has specifically commanded us to study and grow.

Lesson Theme

Study is not confined to a classroom or a time period. God wants us to be continually learning and growing our entire lives. God has provided us with many things to study: the principles of His Word, the lives of people, and His own attributes.

Lesson Objectives

At the conclusion of the lesson, each student should:

1. Understand the three-fold process of growth—seek, do, teach.

2. Commit themselves to being a lifelong student of God's principles, the lives of great Christians, and God's attributes.
3. Purpose to pursue habits and patterns of learning and growth.

Teaching Outline

Introduction

I. Student of Principles
   A. To seek
   B. To do
   C. To teach

II. Student of People
   A. People from the past
   B. People from the present

III. Student of the Person of God
   A. Attributes of God the Father
   B. Attributes of God the Son
   C. Attributes of God the Holy Spirit

Conclusion

LESSON THREE

A Student of God's Word

Text

2 TIMOTHY 2:15

15 *Study to shew thyself approved unto God, a workman that needeth not to be ashamed, rightly dividing the word of truth.*

Introduction

Being in the field of education for over three decades has given me the privilege to work with all types of students. Our typical idea of a student is "one who goes to school," but learning should not stop with graduation. We all should continue to be students our entire lives.

In the sunset years of his life, the Apostle Paul requested Timothy to come to him in the prison and bring "*the books, but especially the parchments*" (2 Timothy 4:13). Although Paul was mature in his faith and had been used by God to write much of the New Testament, he still felt the need to continue learning.

God specifically commands us to study.

2 Timothy 2:15
15 Study to shew thyself approved unto God, a workman that needeth not to be ashamed, rightly dividing the word of truth.

If we are to obey God and remain students for life, we must understand what we should study.

I. Student of Principles

Every Christian should be a student of the principles of the Word of God. The purpose in studying God's principles is two–fold: change and growth. God wants to conform us into the image of Christ, which requires change, and He also wants us to grow to spiritual maturity. There can be no genuine growth without inner change.

We see an excellent example of the growth process outlined in the life of Ezra the scribe.

Ezra 7:10
10 For Ezra had prepared his heart to seek the law of the Lord, and to do it, and to teach in Israel statutes and judgments.

Ezra followed a three-phase process—seek, do, teach.

A. To seek

We begin by seeking God's Word, for we cannot effectively obey and teach the Bible until we first know it in a real and personal way. We must allow God's Word to penetrate our hearts and thus permeate our lives.

Psalm 119:11
11 Thy word have I hid in mine heart, that I might not sin against thee.

TEACHING TIP

(Note: Bring a tea bag and hot water for this illustration. If your class is small enough and your meeting room conducive, you could make tea for everyone to sip during class.)

For hot water to be made into tea, one must allow the tea bag to "steep," to remain in the water for several minutes until the water has thoroughly absorbed its flavor.

When God's Word is allowed to "steep" in our hearts through memorization and meditation, it will change our lives.

Proverbs 4:23

23 *Keep thy heart with all diligence; for out of it are the issues of life.*

The quality of our lives is determined by the quality of our hearts, and that is why we need to hide God's Word in our hearts.

We are blessed in America to have ready access to the Word of God. Yet having it available is not the same as reading it. The one who *does not* read the Word of God is in no better condition than the one who *cannot* read it. In fact, he is in worse condition, because he has the truth accessible to him but ignores it.

Luke 12:48

48 *...For unto whomsoever much is given, of him shall be much required: and to whom men have committed much, of him they will ask the more.*

God warns us that the Bible may not always be so easily accessible.

AMOS 8:11

11 *Behold, the days come, saith the Lord GOD, that I will send a famine in the land, not a famine of bread, nor a thirst for water, but of hearing the words of the LORD:*

ISAIAH 55:6

6 *Seek ye the LORD while he may be found, call ye upon him while he is near:*

We must not waste the opportunities we have to learn the Word of God; rather we must seek it while we have it so abundantly available.

Illustration

A pastor unexpectedly showed up at the door of one of his parishioners for a brief visit. The mother, in an attempt to impress the pastor, turned to her young daughter and asked her to bring "the book that Mommy loves to read." The little girl scurried off and returned beaming, expecting praise as she handed her mother the *TV Guide.*

Our family members know if we are seeking and studying the truths of God's Word!

B. To do

Ezra did not stop with seeking the Word of God—he obeyed it.

JAMES 1:22

22 *But be ye doers of the word, and not hearers only, deceiving your own selves.*

Those who *know* God's truth, but do not *live* God's truth deceive themselves into thinking they are mature

Christians. It is not enough to simply know the Bible; we must live it.

Jesus told a story about two brothers who were told to go to work in their father's vineyard (Matthew 21:28–32). The first son initially refused to go, but afterward he repented and went. The second son obediently answered, "I go, sir," but he never went. Which one of these boys did the will of his father—the one who just talked about it or the one who actually did it?

It wasn't the words that counted; it was the actions. We need to make sure that we are not only seeking the Word of God, but doing it and carrying it out in our daily lives.

Illustration

The great American author Samuel Clemens (better known by his pen name, Mark Twain) said, "It's not the parts of the Bible I don't understand that bother me. It's the parts I *do* understand." He knew that his lifestyle did not reflect the teaching of God's Word. We need to ask God to give us the grace and strength to do the things that we know are right.

Learn the Bible, but don't stop with the learning—live the Bible.

C. To teach

Seeking and obeying God's Word motivates us to teach it to others. What a joy to pass on the blessings we are receiving from our continuing spiritual growth.

Second Chronicles 34 records the account of King Josiah, who repaired the previously neglected temple of God. The repairmen found the Word of God while they were working in the temple. When they brought it to King Josiah, he realized how greatly God's people had failed to live by God's law, so he taught it to them personally. As a result, God sent a great revival that had continuing effects during Josiah's entire life.

2 Chronicles 34:33

33 *And Josiah took away all the abominations out of all the countries that pertained to the children of Israel, and made all that were present in Israel to serve, even to serve the Lord their God. And all his days they departed not from following the Lord, the God of their fathers.*

This revival began with a man who found the Word of God, decided to live by it, and then taught it to others.

If we will also surrender ourselves to teach the Word of God to others, God can do wonderful things in their lives.

Paul gave Timothy a solemn responsibility—to propagate God's Word.

2 Timothy 2:2

2 *And the things that thou hast heard of me among many witnesses, the same commit thou to faithful men, who shall be able to teach others also.*

Paul had poured himself into Timothy, his son in the faith. He now instructed Timothy to pick up the baton of truth and pass on what he had learned to others. But even more, Paul specifically instructed Timothy to pass it on to others who would continue the process. Teaching and learning must never cease.

We are especially responsible to teach the Word of God to our own children.

Deuteronomy 6:6–7

6 *And these words, which I command thee this day, shall be in thine heart:*

7 *And thou shalt teach them diligently unto thy children, and shalt talk of them when thou sittest in thine house, and when thou walkest by the way, and when thou liest down, and when thou risest up.*

David praised God for the heritage he had been given.

Psalm 16:6

6 *The lines are fallen unto me in pleasant places; yea, I have a goodly heritage.*

Can our children say that we have given them a goodly heritage, the legacy of a godly Christian family on which they can model their own families? Teaching God's principles to succeeding generations doesn't stop with our children; we are to teach our grandchildren the Word of God as well.

Deuteronomy 4:9

9 *Only take heed to thyself, and keep thy soul diligently, lest thou forget the things which thine eyes have seen, and lest they depart from thy heart all the days of thy life: but teach them thy sons, and thy sons' sons;*

God's plan is for each generation to influence as many succeeding generations as possible. This is how a Christian family is perpetuated. When one generation fails in this responsibility, the results are devastating. Judges 2:7–12 records how this happens.

Judges 2:7–8, 10–12

*7 And the people served the Lord all the days of Joshua,
and all the days of the elders that outlived Joshua, who had
seen all the great works of the Lord, that he did for Israel.
8 And Joshua the son of Nun, the servant of the Lord,
died, being an hundred and ten years old.
10 And also all that generation were gathered unto their
fathers: and there arose another generation after them,
which knew not the Lord, nor yet the works which he had
done for Israel.
11 And the children of Israel did evil in the sight of the
Lord, and served Baalim:
12 And they forsook the Lord God of their fathers, which
brought them out of the land of Egypt, and followed other
gods, of the gods of the people that were round about them,
and bowed themselves unto them, and provoked the Lord
to anger.*

Joshua led the people of his generation to serve the Lord, but they failed to teach their children in the ways of God. As a result, those of the next generation did not even know the Lord, and they forsook Him to serve idols.

Training our children in the ways of the Lord is commanded throughout the Bible.

Proverbs 22:6

6 Train up a child in the way he should go: and when he is old, he will not depart from it.

Ephesians 6:4

4 And, ye fathers, provoke not your children to wrath: but bring them up in the nurture and admonition of the Lord.

What a wonderful opportunity and a fearsome responsibility we have to teach the Word of God to our children! Truly, the future of our nation depends on it, for our children *are* our future.

The wisest man who ever lived (except the Lord Jesus) was Solomon. The book of Proverbs is Solomon's letter to his son, and it is a principle-centered book. Consider a few of the principles taught in the book of Proverbs.

Nearness is likeness. "*He that walketh with wise men shall be wise: but a companion of fools shall be destroyed*" (Proverbs 13:20).

The Word of God is the greatest compilation and repository of wisdom that ever was or ever shall be. "*The fear of the Lord is the beginning of wisdom: and the knowledge of the holy is understanding*" (Proverbs 9:10).

Listening increases learning. "*A wise man will hear, and will increase learning; and a man of understanding shall attain unto wise counsels*" (Proverbs 1:5).

Our own understanding is extremely fallible; we must not rely on self-guidance. "*Trust in the Lord with all thine heart; and lean not unto thine own understanding. In all thy ways acknowledge him, and he shall direct thy paths*" (Proverbs 3:5–6).

TEACHING TIP

Many Christians who have a real desire for wisdom have made it a habit to read from the book of Proverbs on a daily basis. There are 31 chapters, so you can read a chapter or two every day and in this way easily read through the whole book every month.

All throughout Scripture are many other wonderful principles. These are principles that we all need to learn and incorporate into our own lives, and to teach them to others as we have opportunity.

Regardless of our age, we are to be students of the principles found in the Word of God. Like Ezra, we need to seek God's Word, obey God's Word, and teach God's Word to others.

II. Student of People

The diligent student learns all he can from whomever he can. God brings people into our lives so that we can learn from them. From some people we learn what we *ought* to do, and from others we learn what we ought *not* to do.

A. People from the past

Wise is the person who will learn from people of the past. Rich lessons can be learned in the corridors of history. When we find a life well-lived, we should strive to incorporate into our lives the principles from that person's life which honor Christ and which God has blessed.

Scripture gives us numerous illustrations of lives blessed by the hand of God. These testimonies can be shining examples for us. Let's consider a few of these Bible characters and what we can learn from them:

- Gideon's life teaches that through God we can overcome seemingly insurmountable adversity.
- Jonah's life teaches that nothing is too hard for God.
- Moses' experience as a child in an ark of bulrushes in the Nile River teaches that God will

never leave us and that He watches over us no matter how desperate the situation seems to be.

- Hosea's example teaches that we can forgive, regardless of how badly we have been wronged.
- Paul's life teaches that God can use anyone in a great way, regardless of their past.
- Nicodemus' life teaches that, no matter our social standing, we still must be born again.
- Joseph's life teaches that, no matter how dark the night, God will never leave us or forsake us.
- Ruth's life teaches that there is a kinsman Redeemer.

Undoubtedly, God has given us many details about Bible characters for a purpose—that we may look to them as our examples and, in a sense, our tutors and teachers. Paul explained, *"these things were our examples"* (1 Corinthians 10:6).

More recent history also furnishes us with many lives worthy of emulation. Learn from these lives by reading good biographies of great Christians. In addition to reading about preachers and missionaries, study the lives of others who lived exemplary lives for the Lord. R.G. LeTourneau and John Wanamaker, two businessmen who put the Lord first in their lives and businesses, are such men. Others include Eric Liddell (a British Olympic runner who refused to run on the Lord's day) and William Wilberforce (who for twenty years fought to eradicate the scourge of slavery from the British Empire).

One of the best ways that we can learn from people of the past is to ask ourselves questions as we study their lives.

- Why did God include this person's life in Scripture (when studying Bible characters)?
- What truths or principles can I learn from this person's life?
- What in this person's life should I imitate, or what should I avoid?

Asking questions stimulates our minds to specifically articulate how we can learn from those who have gone before.

B. *People from the present*

Greatness is often unnoticed in its own generation. A wise student will strive to learn from those around him. A benefit of learning from our contemporaries is that we can more closely observe their lives and receive direct mentoring.

Scripture points out a specific group we should learn from—our spiritual leaders.

Hebrews 13:7

7 Remember them which have the rule over you, who have spoken unto you the word of God: whose faith follow, considering the end of their conversation.

We are to "follow the faith" of our spiritual leaders today. The word *follow* literally means "to imitate" or "to mimic." *Conversation* is an Old English word that means "manner of life, conduct, behavior." This verse teaches then that we need to pattern our lives after the lives of godly leaders.

1 Corinthians 11:1

1 *Be ye followers of me, even as I also am of Christ.*

We are not to worship our spiritual leaders, but we are to follow them and imitate them as they follow and imitate the Lord. Some of the best examples God has provided are the lives of those around us who have dedicated themselves to the Word of God and are living a life of faith. We should see these men and women as mentors from whom we can learn.

Illustration

Over the last decade of my life, I have been challenged by my pastor, Dr. Paul Chappell, who says, "Keep the main thing the main thing, and the main thing is soulwinning." This oft–repeated statement is backed by his testimony. Month after month and year after year I have seen people that he has personally won to Christ walk the aisle and follow the Lord in believer's baptism.

I have been challenged by our soulwinning pastor, Jerry Ferrso, to make extra time to knock on doors to share the Gospel.

As a teenager, I was challenged by my youth pastor, who exemplified both faithfulness and loyalty.

What have you learned from your spiritual leaders?

Daniel's sterling character was noticed by those around him. Those who sought to find fault in him realized they could only create it by outlawing the prayer life Daniel lived daily (Daniel 6:10). People who watched Daniel's life, believers and unbelievers, were given a godly example. Even while Daniel was still alive, he was ranked with such heroes as Noah and Job (Ezekiel 14:14, 20).

Illustration

John and Charles Wesley impacted two continents for the Lord Jesus Christ. Their lives were a picture of constancy and consistency in areas such as Bible study, prayer, and care for the unfortunate and needy. They were willing to have intense times of fasting and prayer as they called out for God's Spirit and revival to fall upon the land. Living with such consistency, the Wesleys were often ridiculed for their methodical lives.

Just as people watched and studied the Wesleys, people are watching and studying our lives as well.

This principle of learning from others works two ways. If we understand that people are watching us, we will want to be sure to make the right choices. We ought to pause and ask the question, "What do people learn from watching *my* life?"

Studying the lives of great servants of the Lord, past and present, enables us to learn and grow from their successes and failures. It provides opportunities to be mentored and challenged. And it reminds us of the care we must take in the example we give and the legacy we pass down.

III. Student of the Person of God

God Himself is our primary teacher. When we learn God's attributes and allow God to make us more like Himself, we can more clearly and fully show Him to a lost and dying world.

A. *Attributes of God the Father*

God's attributes include those that belong uniquely to God, such as omniscience (all-knowledge), omnipotence (all-power), and omnipresence (all-present). God also possesses attributes that He specifically instructs us to reflect through our lives.

- Our God is love (1 John 4:8), so we should be loving.
- Our God is just (Isaiah 45:21), so we should be just.
- Our God forgives us (1 John 1:9), so we should forgive others.
- Our God is faithful (1 Corinthians 10:13), so we should be faithful.
- Our God is holy (1 Peter 1:16), so we should be holy.

Our lives are to be a reflection of our God, drawing others to see the greatness and goodness of the God we know and serve. Studying the attributes of God enables us both to know Him better and to better understand what He wants us to be.

B. *Attributes of God the Son*

The Lord Jesus Christ was the one and only God-man, and He is our chief example.

1 PETER 2:21

21 For even hereunto were ye called: because Christ also suffered for us, leaving us an example, that ye should follow his steps:

Illustration

Many years ago Charles Sheldon wrote the novel *In His Steps*. The story concerned a pastor who challenged his congregation to live their lives according to the principle, "What would Jesus do?" Surely we could do no better than to do what Jesus would do in every situation.

Yet the only way we will know what Jesus would do in different situations is to study Jesus' life and personal qualities in God's Word. We see, for example, that Jesus always displayed the spirit of kindness to children. To follow His example, we must not view children as irritations, but as people in which to invest and serve.

We see in Jesus total devotion and sacrifice; He was willing to die to self and to give up His own will in order to please His Heavenly Father. And so we need to give our will over to God, as Jesus did.

From the example of Jesus, we also see that we need to take time to be alone with God. Time and time again, He would go alone up to a mountain to pray or into a desert place to pray and be alone with God. If Jesus needed to spend time alone with God, how much more do we!

We see how Jesus answered the temptations of Satan with the Word of God and how He did not retaliate or even open His mouth when personally attacked. We can learn from His example how to respond to a lost and often hostile world.

The life of our Lord, unlike any other man, provides a flawless example for us to follow, and God's purpose for us is to conform us to the image of Christ.

Romans 8:28–29

28 *And we know that all things work together for good to them that love God, to them who are the called according to his purpose.*

29 *For whom he did foreknow, he also did predestinate to be conformed to the image of his Son, that he might be the firstborn among many brethren.*

We learn about Christ by reading the Bible, and He uses His Word to transform us into His likeness.

2 Corinthians 3:18

18 *But we all, with open face beholding as in a glass the glory of the Lord, are changed into the same image from glory to glory, even as by the Spirit of the Lord.*

We need to study the attributes of the Lord Jesus and strive daily to be more and more like Him.

C. Attributes of God the Holy Spirit

The Holy Spirit has many names, and each of them describe His attributes. Among His many names, my favorite is "Comforter."

John 16:7

7 *Nevertheless I tell you the truth; It is expedient for you that I go away: for if I go not away, the Comforter will not come unto you; but if I depart, I will send him unto you.*

We find this name for the Holy Spirit used three additional times in the Gospel of John—14:16, 14:26, and 15:26.

William J. Kirkpatrick wrote a well-known hymn called "The Comforter Has Come":

> The Comforter has come, the Comforter
> has come!
> The Holy Ghost from Heav'n, the Father's
> promise giv'n;
> O spread the tidings 'round, wherever man
> is found
> The Comforter has come!

The Holy Spirit is also spoken of as a guide.

John 16:13

13 *Howbeit when he, the Spirit of truth, is come, he will guide you into all truth: for he shall not speak of himself; but whatsoever he shall hear, that shall he speak: and he will shew you things to come.*

The Holy Spirit helps us live for God.

Isaiah 30:21

21 *And thine ears shall hear a word behind thee, saying, This is the way, walk ye in it, when ye turn to the right hand, and when ye turn to the left.*

Ezekiel 36:27

27 *And I will put my spirit within you, and cause you to walk in my statutes, and ye shall keep my judgments, and do them.*

We need to study the qualities of the Holy Spirit and then allow Him to minister to others through us. Through the Holy Spirit's working in our lives, we can comfort others, guide others in the ways of the Lord, and help others live for the Lord.

We could study our entire lifetimes and never scratch the surface of discovering God's infinite goodness and greatness. Yet the more we study Him, the better we will know Him and be like Him.

Conclusion

Study is not confined to a classroom or a time period. God wants us to be continually learning and growing our entire life. God has provided us with many things to study: the principles of His Word, the lives of people, and His own attributes.

Reading, meditating, and studying must be a conscious choice. These activities most definitely run contrary to our carnal natures; by nature we want to be entertained and to be at rest. The serious student, however, will schedule time to study and develop habits conducive to learning. Set aside time every day to meet with the Lord and to study His Word for His principles. Search for His characteristics, and ask Him to transform you into His image. Read biographies, and learn from your spiritual leaders. Train yourself to ask questions as you study and to apply what you learn.

As God's children, may we be obedient to His command to "*Study to shew thyself approved unto God*" (2 Timothy 2:15).

Study Questions

1. What did Paul request from Timothy that indicated that he felt the need to continue learning?
   Paul requested Timothy to come to him in the prison and bring "the books, but especially the parchments" (2 Timothy 4:13).

2. What is the two-fold purpose in studying God's principles?
   The two-fold purpose for studying God's principles is change and growth. God wants to conform us into the image of Christ, which requires change, and God wants us to grow to spiritual maturity.

3. What questions should one ask when studying the lives of other people?
   Why did God include them in Scripture (when studying Bible characters)? What truths or principles can I learn from their lives? What in their lives should I imitate, or what should I avoid?

4. Even though we could study our entire lifetimes and never scratch the surface of discovering God's infinite goodness and greatness, why should we study His attributes?
   The more we study the attributes of God, the better we will know Him and be like Him.

5. Our lesson made the statement, "We must not waste the opportunities we have to learn the Word of God, but seek it while we have it so abundantly available." What opportunities do you have to learn the Word of God?
   Answers will vary, but could include: daily quiet time, Sunday school and church attendance, family devotions, Scripture memorization.

6. What biblical principles do you need to teach your children? What other opportunities do you have to teach God's principles?
   Answers will vary.

7. What specific qualities can you learn from the spiritual leaders God has given you?
   Answers will vary.

8. What habits or patterns do you need to develop to become a diligent student of God's Word?
   Answers will vary.

Memory Verse

2 Timothy 2:15

15 *Study to shew thyself approved unto God, a workman that needeth not to be ashamed, rightly dividing the word of truth.*

LESSON FOUR

A Soldier

Text

2 TIMOTHY 2:1–4

1 *Thou therefore, my son, be strong in the grace that is in
Christ Jesus.*
2 *And the things that thou hast heard of me among many
witnesses, the same commit thou to faithful men, who shall be
able to teach others also.*
3 *Thou therefore endure hardness, as a good soldier of
Jesus Christ.*
4 *No man that warreth entangleth himself with the affairs
of this life; that he may please him who hath chosen him to be
a soldier.*

Overview

The Bible describes the Christian life as a battle, and we as soldiers are privileged to serve under the greatest Captain ever—with an assured victory! We should be motivated to the highest standard of excellence.

Lesson Theme

As soldiers for the Lord Jesus Christ, we must be strong, getting the proper spiritual diet and exercise. We must be single-minded, enduring hardness and resisting distractions. We must be secure, understanding our position, our destination, and our commission.

Lesson Objectives

At the conclusion of the lesson, each student should:

1. Understand the reality of spiritual warfare.
2. Commit themselves to the disciplines that contribute to strength and focus.
3. Purpose to give Christ faithful obedience to the end.

Teaching Outline

Introduction

- I. A Strong Soldier
  - A. Diet
  - B. Exercise
- II. A Single-minded Soldier
  - A. Endures hardness
  - B. Remains free of entanglement
  - C. Obeys his Commanding Officer
- III. A Secure Soldier
  - A. Position
  - B. Destination
  - C. Commission

Conclusion

LESSON FOUR

A Soldier

Text

2 TIMOTHY 2:1–4

1 *Thou therefore, my son, be strong in the grace that is in Christ Jesus.*

2 *And the things that thou hast heard of me among many witnesses, the same commit thou to faithful men, who shall be able to teach others also.*

3 *Thou therefore endure hardness, as a good soldier of Jesus Christ.*

4 *No man that warreth entangleth himself with the affairs of this life; that he may please him who hath chosen him to be a soldier.*

Introduction

A good soldier follows the commands of his leader to win a military victory. He is faithful to the end, whether in victory or defeat, life or death. He does his duty regardless of circumstances and in spite of difficulties.

The Bible describes the Christian life as a battle. Unfortunately, many Christians do not realize that they are living in a war zone every day. Because they cannot see the battle that surrounds them, they doubt its reality.

Ephesians 6:12

12 *For we wrestle not against flesh and blood, but against principalities, against powers, against the rulers of the darkness of this world, against spiritual wickedness in high places.*

Wrestling involves an intense struggle for supremacy.

Illustration

Wrestling was extremely important in the Greco-Roman world. During the time of the Apostle Paul, the outcome of a wrestling match could involve serious consequences. The winner received praise, adulation, and rewards, while the loser could have his eyes gouged out, or worse. With so much at stake, it only made sense for each contestant to prepare himself in every way possible and give the struggle his absolute best effort.

More is at stake in the unseen spiritual warfare than any wrestler ever faced. Second Timothy 2 and Ephesians 6 both admonish the Christian to prepare himself with the armor of God and to give his all in the spiritual battle he faces daily.

Paul admonished Timothy, "*fight the good fight of faith*" (1 Timothy 6:12). Our text verses describe the qualities of a successful soldier. Our lives must contain these qualities for us to be good soldiers of Jesus Christ.

I. A Strong Soldier

A soldier must be strong and fit for the battle, and a Christian soldier is no exception.

2 Timothy 2:1

1 *Thou therefore, my son, be strong in the grace that is in Christ Jesus.*

No one sets a goal to be weak. People want to be strong and healthy, and the increasing size of the fitness and diet industries reflects this. Fitness centers, health food stores, and vitamin shops can be found everywhere. Everyone agrees that diet and regular exercise are key to strength and health.

Illustration

New military recruits are required to take several weeks of basic training, or "boot camp." A primary goal in this training is to make the recruit physically fit and strong, disciplined, and able to endure. This training prepares the recruit for a later service assignment.

Anything left to itself eventually decays, falls apart, and atrophies. A garden will fill up with weeds, a house will fall apart, a car will eventually cease to run. Unless we put effort into keeping ourselves strong and healthy, our physical condition will inevitably deteriorate. Even so, our spiritual strength will deteriorate if neglected. To be strong Christian soldiers, we must carefully maintain our spiritual diet and exercise for strength in spiritual warfare.

A. Diet

The Word of God is often compared to food.

Job 23:12

12 *Neither have I gone back from the commandment of his lips; I have esteemed the words of his mouth more than my necessary food.*

Psalm 119:103

103 *How sweet are thy words unto my taste! yea, sweeter than honey to my mouth!*

Jeremiah 15:16

16 *Thy words were found, and I did eat them; and thy word was unto me the joy and rejoicing of mine heart: for I am called by thy name, O Lord God of hosts.*

1 Peter 2:2

2 *As newborn babes, desire the sincere milk of the word, that ye may grow thereby:*

Serious athletes understand the importance of ingesting the right kind of food. They regularly measure calories and keep careful totals of protein counts. They also monitor their diet for other nutrients to ensure their bones and muscles can be strengthened and sustained.

Illustration

A number of years ago, a father by the name of Marv Marinovich, a former NFL lineman, decided that he was going to help his son Todd develop into a great athlete. He trained him in a very unique way. They ate only from an all-natural menu. They never ate a McDonald's hamburger or consumed any type of sugar or soft drinks. Todd succeeded well enough to play quarterback for the University of Southern California and to be drafted in the first round by the Oakland Raiders.

Just as the proper diet is essential for the athlete who wants to succeed, the proper diet is important for the soldier who must be in good physical shape to carry out the orders of his superiors. The Christian soldier must be spiritually fit to serve his Master to the fullest. Thus, he needs a proper diet—the meat of the Word of God.

The world is quick to offer a full selection of junk food that may be light and tasty—yet gives no nutrition. It looks good, but it is not beneficial. Many times it is actually harmful. This is true in both the physical realm (with the multitude of fast–food restaurants and microwave dinners available) and the spiritual realm.

Many leaders in the self-help and success industry claim to be spiritual leaders, but if their advice is not solidly based on the Word of God, it will lead you in the wrong direction. Watch your diet—physically, spiritually, mentally, and emotionally!

Spend time daily feeding on God's Word. Don't just read to check something off your to–do list, but read to learn. Take the time to really think about what you have read, and let God work in your mind, heart, and life.

Don't just settle for "Twinkie" devotions, where you quickly read a verse or two and say a short, routine prayer. That won't help you grow in the Lord.

Think about a cow chewing her cud. She does not hurry, and she gets all she can out of that mouthful of food. We need to do the same with the Word of God.

B. Exercise

Usually the words *diet* and *exercise* are paired. If we eat and do not exercise, we tend to expand in an unhealthy manner! Exercise without eating properly will not be good for us either. Regular exercise must accompany a proper diet. How can we, as soldiers of Christ, exercise in the spiritual sense?

First, we must exercise our ***faith***. Abraham is an example of a man who exercised his faith. Faith is extremely important because the Christian life is lived by faith, and God instructs us to walk by faith in every area of our life.

ROMANS 4:20
20 He staggered not at the promise of God through unbelief; but was strong in faith, giving glory to God;

2 CORINTHIANS 5:7
7 (For we walk by faith, not by sight:)

ROMANS 14:23
23 ...whatsoever is not of faith is sin.

Faith is like a muscle; it does not grow naturally—it must be exercised. As we exercise in living by faith, it will become a habit. We establish bad habits by the repetition of wrong actions, and we establish good habits by the repetition of right actions.

Exercise your faith by choosing to trust God—even in the face of difficult circumstances or uncertainty. Exercise your faith by reading and believing the promises of God. Exercise your faith by obeying the commands of God, trusting that He will bless your obedience.

We need to exercise ourselves in ***right living***. By doing this, Paul testified of a clear conscience to Felix.

ACTS 24:16
16 And herein do I exercise myself, to have always a conscience void of offence toward God, and toward men.

Paul practiced right living so that he would have no regrets toward either God or his fellow man. No matter what the situation or what the difficulties, he exercised himself to do the right thing every time.

Finally, we need to exercise ourselves in ***godliness***.

1 Timothy 4:7–8

7 *But refuse profane and old wives' fables, and exercise thyself rather unto godliness.*

8 *For bodily exercise profiteth little: but godliness is profitable unto all things, having promise of the life that now is, and of that which is to come.*

This need to exercise yourself in having the proper attitude toward God and in giving Him the respect and honor He deserves does not come naturally—it will take work.

When evaluating your spiritual diet and exercise, keep in mind that there is always room for growth. God does not expect from a baby Christian what He expects from a mature Christian.

Hebrews 5:14

14 *But strong meat belongeth to them that are of full age, even those who by reason of use have their senses exercised to discern both good and evil.*

None of us want to live our entire Christian life on a child's level. We need a proper spiritual diet and consistent exercise to grow.

2 Peter 3:18

18 *But grow in grace, and in the knowledge of our Lord and Saviour Jesus Christ. To him be glory both now and for ever. Amen.*

A soldier must be strong. Choose to make the diet and exercise that will make you strong in the Lord part of your daily routines.

II. A Single-minded Soldier

A soldier must also be single-minded.

2 TIMOTHY 2:3–5
3 *Thou therefore endure hardness, as a good soldier of Jesus Christ.*
4 *No man that warreth entangleth himself with the affairs of this life; that he may please him who hath chosen him to be a soldier.*
5 *And if a man also strive for masteries, yet is he not crowned, except he strive lawfully.*

What does it take to become a single-minded soldier? What are the characteristics of a single-minded soldier?

A. Endures hardness

Hardships are part of a soldier's job description.

2 TIMOTHY 2:3
3 *Thou therefore endure hardness, as a good soldier of Jesus Christ.*

The songwriter expressed this truth so well when he asked, "Shall I be carried to the skies on flow'ry beds of ease, while others fight to win the prize and sail through bloody seas?"

We are in a battle, and it's not easy. Paul encouraged us to *"press toward the mark"* (Philippians 3:14). Success will take effort, determination, and endurance.

Illustration

An intense event called the Crucible marks the end of the basic training of a United States Marine. The Military News Network website describes the Crucible like this: "The Crucible marks a final test of everything Marine recruits have learned. Here, they will experience sleep deprivation, food rationing, and a series of intense mental and physical tests that will put an exclamation point on their time in recruit training. By the time recruits take on the Crucible, they normally have about eleven weeks of solid training behind them, and it will all be needed. Tired and hungry, they must work together to overcome extreme challenges or experience the bitterness of failure as a platoon." [Source: http://www.militarynewsnetwork.com/join-marines.htm]

A mother of a marine gives a few more details: "Fifty-four grueling hours—forty–mile hike stopping at different stations—learning survival and teamwork—four hours sleep total—three meals total. Will be one of the hardest things ever done."

Think of the monumental level of endurance required of a recruit in order to make it through the Crucible and earn the right to become a United States Marine! A soldier is expected to "endure hardness."

As Christian soldiers, God wants us to demonstrate our single-mindedness by enduring hardness. We all enjoy the sweet promises of God—promises of His presence, His protection, His provision. Yet God also promises there will be need for endurance.

2 Timothy 3:12

12 *Yea, and all that will live godly in Christ Jesus shall suffer persecution.*

Matthew 5:10–12

10 *Blessed are they which are persecuted for righteousness' sake: for theirs is the kingdom of heaven.*

11 *Blessed are ye, when men shall revile you, and persecute you, and shall say all manner of evil against you falsely, for my sake.*

12 *Rejoice, and be exceeding glad: for great is your reward in heaven: for so persecuted they the prophets which were before you.*

1 Peter 4:12–13

12 *Beloved, think it not strange concerning the fiery trial which is to try you, as though some strange thing happened unto you:*

13 *But rejoice, inasmuch as ye are partakers of Christ's sufferings; that, when his glory shall be revealed, ye may be glad also with exceeding joy.*

So God promises us hardships and afflictions as well as joy and peace. How could we truly know the peace of God were there no unrest for us in the world? How could we have real joy in Christ if there were no earthly sorrow?

John 16:33

33 *These things I have spoken unto you, that in me ye might have peace. In the world ye shall have tribulation: but be of good cheer; I have overcome the world.*

We can remain single-minded by setting ourselves to endure hardness. We have God's own promise that the final victory will be ours as we are faithful to the Lord.

1 Corinthians 15:58

58 *Therefore, my beloved brethren, be ye stedfast, unmoveable, always abounding in the work of the Lord,*

forasmuch as ye know that your labour is not in vain in the Lord.

B. Remains free of entanglement

A single-minded soldier refuses to be distracted by anything that competes with his duty.

2 Timothy 2:4

4 *No man that warreth entangleth himself with the affairs of this life; that he may please him who hath chosen him to be a soldier.*

Illustration

The Tomb of the Unknown Soldier in the Arlington National Cemetery near Washington, D.C. is a monument to those soldiers who gave their lives in service to the United States but whose bodies were not identified. This tomb is guarded twenty-four hours a day, seven days a week.

The sentinel on duty performs his responsibility with great ceremony and utmost precision. He takes twenty-one steps (alluding to the twenty-one-gun salute, the highest honor given any military dignity) across the tomb, turns to face the tomb for twenty-one seconds, turns again and changes his weapon to the outside shoulder, counts another twenty-one seconds, and makes a twenty-one-step return walk. He continues this process until he is relieved at the Guard Change. [Source: http://keneva.com/TombOfTheUnknownSoldierFacts.htm]

This guard allows no distractions to his mission. Weather does not matter. Friends in the crowd watching the ceremony do not matter. If the soldier's nose itches, he waits until he is formally relieved and out of sight to scratch it! No distractions, no entanglements, no personal concerns will keep this soldier from performing his duty.

The world in which we live provides many opportunities for distractions and entanglement. We can become overly concerned with houses, cars, finances, hobbies, and even problems.

TEACHING TIP

Reading missionary biographies of people who literally left all and followed the Lord can be challenging and motivating. Encourage your class to read biographies. If your church has a bookstore or library with such books, this would be a good time to promote them in class. For starters, you can find a list of recommended reading on Pastor Paul Chappell's webpage: http://www.paulchappell.com/2008/10/29/recommended-reading/.

My pastor, Dr. Paul Chappell, often reminds us of the Lord Jesus' words that no man can serve two masters (Matthew 6:24). If we are trying to serve the Lord and ourselves, or the Lord and our finances, or the Lord and our hobbies, we then have two masters. This distraction will make us unstable soldiers.

James 1:8

8 A double minded man is unstable in all his ways.

Free yourself from distractions by keeping your focus on the Lord Himself.

C. Obeys his Commanding Officer

A submitted soldier is an effective soldier.

Matthew 8:8–9

8 *The centurion answered and said, Lord, I am not worthy that thou shouldest come under my roof: but speak the word only, and my servant shall be healed.*

9 *For I am a man under authority, having soldiers under me: and I say to this man, Go, and he goeth; and to another, Come, and he cometh; and to my servant, Do this, and he doeth it.*

Just as the Roman soldiers under this centurion were required to obey, a Christian soldier, likewise, must obey God. The Bible is the manual for the Christian soldier, and spiritual warfare must be conducted according to the guidelines found in the Word of God.

Under battle conditions, there may occasionally be some confusion as to who is in charge, but military progress cannot be made until this confusion is resolved. This is why Christians must be fully aware of just who our Commanding Officer is. As long as we are trying to fight *our* way, we will not be successful for the cause of Christ.

Joshua learned the importance of recognizing God as the supreme commanding officer just before the battle of Jericho. As he stood outside the city, no doubt calculating his plans for battle, he encountered a man with a drawn sword. *"Art thou for us, or for our adversaries?"* (Joshua 5:13) Joshua asked. The answer was humbling: *"Nay; but as captain of the host of the Lord am I now come"* (Joshua 5:14). The Lord, as the rightful captain, then gave Joshua *His* battle plans.

Later in Joshua's life, he reminded the Israelites that they must single-mindedly serve the Lord. He challenged them, "*...choose you this day whom ye will serve*" (Joshua 24:15) and then announced his own choice: "*...as for me and my house, we will serve the Lord.*"

The world prefers to cut corners, doing things the easy way. But success in warfare demands single-minded soldiers. Don't allow your heart to dwell on the hardness of the warfare and become overwhelmed. Instead, concentrate on the goodness of God. Don't become distracted by worldly entanglements. Focus on your duties as a soldier. And don't attempt to fight spiritual battles your way. Submit to your Commanding Officer, and make His pleasure your highest goal.

III. A Secure Soldier

A soldier must understand who he is, where he is headed, and what his responsibilities are. A clear recognition of these things provides the sense of security he needs to focus on his mission.

A. Position

The soldier knows who he is and where he stands—his identity.

Illustration

Every soldier in the United States military is made to believe that he is a member of the "best of the best." His branch of service is the greatest—no question. He is secure in his position.

One of the biggest college football games of the year is the Army-Navy game, pitting the team of the United States Military Academy at West Point, New York (Army), against the United States Naval Academy at Annapolis, Maryland (Navy). These are not necessarily top teams in the national standings, but the game has been nationally televised for many years. The first game in 1890 was won by the Navy. Overall, the Navy leads in the series 53–49 with 7 ties and a seven-game winning streak. Up in the stands, everyone takes sides. They know *exactly* which side they're rooting for! They are secure in their position.

A Christian must be aware of and secure in his position as well. It is a great honor to be a soldier for the King of kings.

B. Destination

A secure soldier knows where he is headed—his destination. Our Commander has clearly told us our final destination—Heaven.

JOHN 14:2–3

2 *In my Father's house are many mansions: if it were not so, I would have told you. I go to prepare a place for you.*
3 *And if I go and prepare a place for you, I will come again, and receive you unto myself; that where I am, there ye may be also.*

A soldier in Christ's army understands his promotion schedule— first suffering, then victory.

2 TIMOTHY 2:12

12 *If we suffer, we shall also reign with him…*

Our future is secure. We truly do know, in the words of Paul Harvey, "the rest of the story."

Illustration

Evangelist Curtis Hutson's body was filled with cancer and racked with pain during his last months on earth before the Lord called him home on March 5, 1995. During his last months, he often sang "I'm On the Winning Side" to remind everyone of the victory Christ promises. Indeed, we are on the winning side, because our ultimate victory is guaranteed.

We have no need to fear the evil one, for we are on the victorious side. We have Christ's own promise that we will someday rule and reign with Him.

C. Commission

Our commission has been given. We have our marching orders, and absolute obedience and faithfulness is required. The same faithfulness required of stewards is required of soldiers.

1 Corinthians 4:2

2 *Moreover it is required in stewards, that a man be found faithful.*

Illustration

The well-known motto of the United States Marine Corps is "*Semper Fidelis,*" which means "Always Faithful."

Commissions are, in reality, commands to fight.

1 Timothy 6:12
12 *Fight the good fight of faith, lay hold on eternal life, whereunto thou art also called, and hast professed a good profession before many witnesses.*

Paul demonstrated personal obedience to his commission.

2 Timothy 4:7
7 *I have fought a good fight, I have finished my course, I have kept the faith:*

In his famous poem, "The Charge of the Light Brigade," Tennyson wrote: "Theirs not to make reply / Theirs not to reason why / Theirs but to do and die."

As soldiers for the Lord, we understand our position—who we are and where we stand. We understand our destination—where we're headed. And we understand our commission—to fight faithfully until the end.

Conclusion

What a privilege to serve in the Lord's army under the greatest Captain ever and with an assured victory! We should be motivated to the highest standard of excellence as a soldier.

We must be strong—getting the proper spiritual diet and exercise. We must be single-minded—enduring hardness and resisting distractions. We must be secure—understanding our position, our destination, and our commission.

Illustration

The sentry guarding the Tomb of the Unknowns does not vary his routine even at night when no one is around. He believes that those buried in that tomb deserve his very best at all hours. How much more does Christ, who was crucified, buried, and rose for us deserve our very best?

Study Questions

1. What two elements are required for strength? What are the spiritual counterparts for the Christian soldier of these elements?
Diet and regular exercise are key to strength and health. A Christian must maintain a regular diet of God's Word and exercise in faith, right living, and godliness.

2. What are the three characteristics of a single-minded soldier?
A single-minded soldier endures hardness, does not allow himself to become entangled with the world, and obeys his Commanding Officer.

3. What is the manual for the Christian soldier?
The Bible is the manual for the Christian soldier.

4. What is the promotion schedule for the Christian soldier?
Our promotion schedule is first suffering, then victory.

5. On a scale of one to ten, where would you place your spiritual strength? What steps can you take to improve your spiritual diet and exercise to increase that number?
Answers will vary, but steps to improve spiritual diet and exercise could include the following: I can become more faithful in my Bible reading and church attendance; I can become accountable to a godly Christian for diligent Scripture memory; I can exercise my faith by obedience to the Lord.

6. What hard circumstances is the Lord allowing in your life right now? What promises can you claim as you patiently endure?
   Answers will vary, but the promises could include the following: Isaiah 40:31, Isaiah 43:2, Psalm 34:15, Psalm 46:1, Romans 8:37–39, 2 Corinthians 12:9, Philippians 4:13, Hebrews 4:16, Proverbs 18:10, and 1 John 5:14–15.

7. What in your life is working to distract you from focusing on your duties as a soldier of Christ? What can you do to keep your focus?
   Answers will vary.

8. Our Captain deserves our very best. In what ways could you increase your level of excellence to give Him your best?
   Answers will vary.

Memory Verse

1 Timothy 6:12

12 *Fight the good fight of faith, lay hold on eternal life, whereunto thou art also called, and hast professed a good profession before many witnesses.*

LESSON FIVE

A Runner in the Christian Race

Text

HEBREWS 12:1–2

1 *Wherefore seeing we also are compassed about with so great a cloud of witnesses, let us lay aside every weight, and the sin which doth so easily beset us, and let us run with patience the race that is set before us,*

2 *Looking unto Jesus the author and finisher of our faith; who for the joy that was set before him endured the cross, despising the shame, and is set down at the right hand of the throne of God.*

Overview

God likens the Christian life to a marathon race. You are a runner, and He is your coach. A successful race is possible for every child of God who submits to the Coach's instructions and runs with patience until he crosses the finish line.

Lesson Theme

As a Christian runner, we have the privilege of running the course Christ has designed for each of us. With a prize before us and our weights behind us, we must strive every day to throw every ounce of our energy into winning the race. When obstacles come, we must meet them with patience; when we are wearied or wounded, we must run to Christ. But if we continue running, we will one day have the joy of crossing the finish line and hearing our Coach and Friend say, "Well done."

Lesson Objectives

At the conclusion of the lesson, each student should:

1. Understand that each Christian has a course set by God on which to run for God's glory.
2. Identify weights that are restricting them from the most effective service for the Lord.
3. Commit to staying in their race until they cross the finish line.

Teaching Outline

Introduction

I. Why to Run
   A. Run because of the witness of heroic runners.
   B. Run to win the prize.

II. How to Run
   A. Run with all you have.
   B. Run within the rules.
   C. Run without weights.
   D. Run with patience.

III. Where to Run
   A. Run to Christ.
   B. Run to the finish line.

Conclusion

LESSON FIVE

A Runner in the Christian Race

Text

HEBREWS 12:1–2

1 *Wherefore seeing we also are compassed about with so*
great a cloud of witnesses, let us lay aside every weight, and the
sin which doth so easily beset us, and let us run with patience
the race that is set before us,
2 *Looking unto Jesus the author and finisher of our faith; who*
for the joy that was set before him endured the cross, despising
the shame, and is set down at the right hand of the throne
of God.

Introduction

God likens the Christian life to a marathon race. You are a runner, and He is your coach. A successful race is possible for every child of God who submits to the coach's instructions and runs with patience until he crosses the finish line.

I. Why to Run

What is the motivation of the runner in the Christian race?

A. Run because of the witness of heroic runners.

Hebrews 11 has often been called "God's hall of faith" because this chapter highlights many of God's faithful runners. Notice the common denominator in the race these heroes ran.

- Able offered a blood sacrifice by faith.
- Enoch pleased God by faith.
- Noah built the ark by faith.
- Abraham obeyed God and moved to Canaan by faith.
- Sarah delivered Isaac as a ninety-year-old woman by faith.
- Abraham offered up Isaac by faith.
- Isaac and Jacob blessed their sons by faith.
- Joseph encouraged Israel to return to the Promised Land by faith.
- Moses' parents hid Moses by faith.
- Moses chose to suffer affliction with his people rather than enjoy the pleasures of sin by faith.
- Moses led the Israelites through the wilderness and instructed them to keep the Passover by faith.
- Rahab spared the lives of the Israelite spies by faith.

Hebrews 12:1 indicates that the heroes of faith mentioned in Hebrews 11 peer over Heaven's portals calling to us and cheering us on in the race God has set before us. And their testimony says to all of us, "What God did for me, He will do for you, too!"

Running the Christian race is not accomplished by special talent, reserved for select few, but rather by ordinary people who have faith in an extraordinary God.

Illustration

Hudson Taylor was an English missionary in China for over fifty years. Through his labors, thousands of Chinese were saved, and many other missionaries came to China. Our tendency when looking at such success in another Christian's race is to think, "Wow, he must have really been a super-Christian!" Taylor, however, knew better. He explained, "God is not looking for men of great faith, only some common souls like you or me...willing to trust in His great faithfulness."

Those listed in Hebrews 11 were common people who were willing to trust in God's great faithfulness. We, too, can exercise our faith when we are willing to simply obey God and run our race, trusting Him to faithfully meet our needs until we reach the finish line.

As you run your race by faith, God will work in your life. And you will then have a testimony to share with others and encourage them as they run their Christian race.

Illustration

A 1954 edition of London's BBC Newspaper ran the following story:

"Roger Bannister, a 25-year-old British medical student, has become the first man to run a mile in less than four minutes.

"His time was 3 minutes 59.4 seconds, achieved at the Iffley Road track in Oxford and watched by about 3,000 spectators."

What is significant to note is that just forty-six days after Bannister broke the 4-minute mile, his new record was broken, and many since then have run a sub-4-minute mile. (The current record is 3:43.13 minutes, set by Hicham El Guerrouj.)

What men had been trying to do for years was spurred forward by one man's accomplishment. When you run your Christian race by faith, other Christians are encouraged to press on in their race.

B. Run to win the prize.

Athletes are motivated by winning. Paul freely spoke of the crowns he wanted to obtain for the glory of God.

1 Corinthians 9:24–25

24 *Know ye not that they which run in a race run all, but one receiveth the prize? So run, that ye may obtain.*
25 *And every man that striveth for the mastery is temperate in all things. Now they do it to obtain a corruptible crown; but we an incorruptible.*

We know that Paul suffered greatly in his service for the Lord. In 2 Corinthians (the most autobiographical of all of Paul's epistles), he lists some of these difficulties.

2 Corinthians 11:24–28

24 *Of the Jews five times received I forty stripes save one.*

25 Thrice was I beaten with rods, once was I stoned, thrice I suffered shipwreck, a night and a day I have been in the deep;
26 In journeyings often, in perils of waters, in perils of robbers, in perils by mine own countrymen, in perils by the heathen, in perils in the city, in perils in the wilderness, in perils in the sea, in perils among false brethren;
27 In weariness and painfulness, in watchings often, in hunger and thirst, in fastings often, in cold and nakedness.
28 Beside those things that are without, that which cometh upon me daily, the care of all the churches.

Even one of these sufferings would discourage the average Christian from continuing his race. Why then did Paul continue? Why did he press on in ministry, even when his very life was threatened?

Philippians 3:14
14 I press toward the mark for the prize of the high calling of God in Christ Jesus.

Paul kept his eyes on the prize ahead. When his body was racked with pain or sagging with weariness, the prize motivated him to press on. When danger lurked ominously near or persecutors assaulted him, the prize motivated him to press on. When he was hungry or cold, lonely or burdened, the prize motivated Paul to press on.

As a runner in the Christian race, keep your eyes on the prize ahead. There will be times when you will want to quit, times when it doesn't seem worthwhile to continue, but remembering the prize will give you courage to press on.

Even Jesus was strengthened to endure the Cross because He focused on the joy that was set before Him.

Hebrews 12:2

2 *Looking unto Jesus the author and finisher of our faith; who for the joy that was set before him endured the cross, despising the shame, and is set down at the right hand of the throne of God.*

One day, every Christian will see Jesus face to face, and what a joy it will be to have successfully finished our race and hear Him say, "*Well done, thou good and faithful servant...enter thou into the joy of thy lord*" (Matthew 25:21).

Paul, who knew all about the hardships of the race, calls out to us cheerfully and tenaciously, "*So run, that ye may obtain*" (1 Corinthians 9:24). You will never win the prize if you don't step on the race track or if you quit because of difficulties. Run to win the prize!

II. How to Run

Running is an intense sport that requires diligent discipline and thorough training. An untrained runner cannot get up the morning of an Olympic competition and decide then to compete! He must learn to run properly to even qualify for the race.

God has given us specific instructions on running our Christian race. When we follow His directions, we are equipped to win the race.

A. Run with all you have.

Runners involve their entire self in winning their race.

Illustration

A runner's effort extends far beyond moving his legs. When he runs, his heart speed increases to give his blood needed oxygen, his lungs work to bring in all the oxygen possible, and his muscles counter-balance each other to propel him forward. The runner's entire body is contributing to the goal of winning the race.

The runner who only gives half-hearted effort is not the winner of a competitive race. From grueling workouts to the race itself, runners must give concentrated focus and effort to improvement.

Half-hearted effort is ineffective in the Christian race as well. Jim Elliot, a missionary to Ecuador who was martyred at the age of twenty-eight said, "Wherever you are, be all there. Live to the hilt every situation you believe to be the will of God." This is good advice for all of us. Give one hundred percent running the race God has set before you.

Colossians 3:23

23 And whatsoever ye do, do it heartily, as to the Lord, and not unto men;

Illustration

In every school there are students who dislike Physical Education (P.E.) class. Perhaps you remember the ones who only ran because they were *made* to run. And even then, they gave just enough effort to keep the P.E. instructor off their back.

Some Christians seem to approach the Christian life the same way. When they should be expending themselves to serve the Lord and others, they hold back, reserving their strength for selfish pursuits. We all must remember that Christ is worthy of our all! He made us and purchased us with His blood. How could we withhold anything from Him?

B. Run within the rules.

Just as there are codes for running a race, including qualifications for entering the race as well as winning the race, even so God has given us instructions for running the Christian race.

We only enter the race by trusting in the sacrifice Jesus paid for our sins.

John 3:36
36 He that believeth on the Son hath everlasting life: and he that believeth not the Son shall not see life; but the wrath of God abideth on him.

Once we have trusted Jesus as our Saviour, we have the Holy Spirit to guide us in following the course God has laid out before us. The Holy Spirit guides us in applying God's instructions for living the Christian life (John 16:13).

God also gives us His grace—the desire and the power to obey and follow Him.

Philippians 2:13
13 For it is God which worketh in you both to will and to do of his good pleasure.

God's grace gives every Christian runner the ability to navigate the race track of his life successfully. From God's Word we learn how to live a victorious Christian life, and through God's grace, we are empowered to do it.

Illustration

In 1980, for the first time ever, a woman was the first to cross the finish line for the Boston Marathon. But shortly after Rosie Ruiz accepted her gold medal and her victory laurels, officials questioned her win. They wondered why she was not present in any of the video footage of the race? And why had none of the checkpoint monitors seen her pass?

After several onlookers admitted to having seen Rosie enter the race during the last mile, she was stripped of her marathon title, and a larger medal was given to the real winner, Jacqueline Gareau.

Sometimes we are tempted to only *appear* to live according to God's instructions. If others think we "have it all together," that is enough for us. Like Rosie Ruiz, we may have apparent victory, but we will ultimately encounter defeat. Rosie had a moment of impressive victory, but she is now famous for cheating. Remember that records mean nothing if they do not reflect reality. God's desire is that our outward actions would be a reflection of the work He is doing in our hearts.

Many have an outward show of godliness, but the real Christian race is run from the heart and *then* expressed outwardly.

C. Run without weights.

Have you ever seen a marathon runner arrive on the race track with a winter coat, heavy boots, and a backpack filled with snacks? Probably not. While there is nothing wrong with these items, a runner works to make himself as light as possible. When he is going to race, he will choose lightweight clothing and set aside anything that would weigh him down while he is running.

Hebrews 12:1 admonishes the Christian runner to do the same: "*…let us lay aside every weight, and the sin which doth so easily beset us….*" A *weight* is anything that holds you back from most effectively and efficiently running the race God has set before you. It may not be *sinful,* but if it restricts you from running your race, it is *foolish.*

Weights for the Christian runner may include activities, habits, or relationships that pull his heart back from pursuing Christ. Paul chose to set aside anything that would restrict him from pressing forward for Christ.

Philippians 3:13–14
13 *Brethren, I count not myself to have apprehended: but this one thing I do, forgetting those things which are behind, and reaching forth unto those things which are before,*
14 *I press toward the mark for the prize of the high calling of God in Christ Jesus.*

D. Run with patience.

If you are not a runner, you may not think of the words *run* and *patience* in the same sentence. After all, if you're running, you want to get somewhere fast! But if you've invested your time and energy in grueling practices and willed yourself to the finish line on a race track, you understand the importance of patience in running.

Winning a race requires the intensity of running *and* the determination of patience. Without patience to train and press on to the finish line, even the most talented runners would never win.

Illustration

Born prematurely at four and a half pounds, no one would have guessed the future of Wilma Rudolf. At age four, she contracted polio, which twisted her left leg and foot and required her to wear braces. Doctors were confident that she would never walk again.

Taking advantage of any shred of hope, the doctors instructed Wilma's mother on how to massage Wilma's leg to prevent her from remaining permanently crippled. These massages were administered faithfully.

During a routine doctor visit, Wilma shocked her doctor when she removed her heavy brace and walked across the room without it. She then disclosed her secret—persistently and painfully, she had forced herself to walk a little each day. This was the turning point for Wilma. Soon, through patience and persistence, she was running.

At age 16, Wilma competed in the 1956 Olympics and returned home with a bronze medal in the 4 x 100-meter relay. Four years later, she returned from the 1960 Olympics with three gold medals—the 100 meter, 200 meter, and 4 x 100 meter relays.

Wilma's life demonstrates the necessity of patience in running a race. Without the patience to willingly endure pain, Wilma would never have walked without her brace, and she certainly would never have competed in the Olympic games.

Patience in a race is the ability to endure until the finish line. It is the inner strength to refuse to become frustrated and quit when one is exhausted or cramping or injured.

Perhaps you're experiencing difficulties and have been tempted to fall out of your Christian race. Don't give up. Instead, grow in patience!

HEBREWS 10:35–36
35 *Cast not away therefore your confidence, which hath great recompence of reward.*
36 *For ye have need of patience, that, after ye have done the will of God, ye might receive the promise.*

When situations come into our lives that require us to develop patience, we mature spiritually.

JAMES 1:3–4
3 *Knowing this, that the trying of your faith worketh patience.*
4 *But let patience have her perfect work, that ye may be perfect and entire, wanting nothing.*

The runner has patience to continue his race because he remembers the end. He knows he will not run indefinitely. By running with patience, he will reach the finish line and victory.

The Christian runner, too, is encouraged when he remembers that as he trusts the Lord with patience, at the end of every trial, God has blessings. Trials don't last forever, but they do yield great joys.

JAMES 5:11
11 *Behold, we count them happy which endure. Ye have heard of the patience of Job, and have seen the end of the Lord; that the Lord is very pitiful, and of tender mercy.*

III. Where to Run

The fastest, strongest, most agile runner will never win if he is on the wrong race track. Even proper breathing and technique, developed through hours of training, accomplishes nothing if he reaches the wrong finish line.

As Christians, we must be careful that we run the race *Christ* has set before us rather than choosing our own direction. We want to reach the proper finish line.

A. Run to Christ.

During the earthly ministry of Jesus, multitudes ran to Him and found that He could meet their every need.

Mark 5:6
6 *But when he saw Jesus afar off, he ran and worshipped him,*

Mark 6:33
33 *And the people saw them departing, and many knew him, and ran afoot thither out of all cities, and outwent them, and came together unto him.*

Mark 6:55–56
55 *And ran through that whole region round about, and began to carry about in beds those that were sick, where they heard he was.*
56 *And whithersoever he entered, into villages, or cities, or country, they laid the sick in the streets, and besought him that they might touch if it were but the border of his garment: and as many as touched him were made whole.*

Jesus always had the answer for those who came to Him. Their running was never in vain. When you have a need or difficulty, your best source of help is Christ. Run to Him in prayer bringing your troubles to Him. Run to Him always—in joy, sorrow, sickness, health, need, praise. Jesus is a Friend that *"sticketh closer than a brother"* (Proverbs 18:24).

Some run to Christ, but others run in another direction.

Proverbs 6:18

18 An heart that deviseth wicked imaginations, feet that be swift in running to mischief,

In what direction are your feet headed? Are you running *to* Christ or *away* from Him?

B. Run to the finish line.

Runners have one goal in mind—the finish line. They are willing to endure fatigue, pain, and heat just to cross the line—even if they collapse on the other side in exhaustion.

Shortly before Paul's death, he had the distinct joy of writing to Timothy, *"I have fought a good fight, I have finished my course, I have kept the faith: Henceforth there is laid up for me a crown of righteousness, which the Lord, the righteous judge, shall give me at that day: and not to me only, but unto all them also that love his appearing"* (2 Timothy 4:7–8).

Illustration

During the 1968 Olympics, held in Mexico City, Tanzania's marathon runner, John Stephen Akhwari, demonstrated to the world the significance of crossing the finish line. During the race, he fell, cutting and dislocating his knee. Spectators expected to see him step to the sidelines and watch the remaining competitors finish the race. But John stood up and continued down the track. Other runners quickly passed him. It was obvious now that he would never win the race—even he must have seen that.

While John struggled along the track, gritting his teeth against the pain, the first runner crossed the line, then the second, and the third. When John finally limped across the finish line over an hour later, only a few spectators remained. Among the spectators was a reporter.

"What made you continue?" the reporter asked. "You surely knew you would never win."

"My country," John explained, "did not send me to Mexico City to start the race. They sent me to finish."

There are many Christians who were terrific starters in their race, but sadly, they are now on the sidelines. Perhaps they were wounded by criticism, crippled by fear, or devastated by tragedy. Some have simply grown weary of running. Whatever the reason, they have chosen not to press on to the finish line.

If you are resting by the sidelines, let me encourage you to get back in the race. Finish strong for the glory of God. Run to Jesus for healing and strength, and continue on the track of victory!

Galatians 6:9

9 *And let us not be weary in well doing: for in due season we shall reap, if we faint not.*

Paul, who endured many "track wounds," didn't look at the bruises, broken bones, or scars. Instead he looked with joy to the finish line.

Acts 20:24

24 *But none of these things move me, neither count I my life dear unto myself, so that I might finish my course with*

joy, and the ministry, which I have received of the Lord Jesus, to testify the gospel of the grace of God.

May each of us have the joy of crossing the finish line and finding ourselves in the arms of our Saviour!

Conclusion

As a Christian runner, we have the privilege of running the course He has designed for each of us. With a prize before us and our weights behind us, we must strive every day to throw every ounce of our energy into winning the race. When obstacles come, we must meet them with patience; when we are wearied or wounded, we must run to Christ. For if we continue running, we will one day have the joy of crossing the finish line and hearing our Coach and Friend say, "Well done."

Study Questions

1. What are two reasons given in this lesson to run the Christian race?
   Run because of the witness of heroic runners, and run to win the prize.

2. How does it affect other Christian's lives when you run your Christian race by faith?
   Other Christians are encouraged to press on in their race.

3. What gives the runner patience to continue his race? How does this relate to running the Christian race?
   The runner has patience to continue his race because he remembers the end. The Christian runner is encouraged when he remembers that at the end of every trial, God has blessings.

4. What is the one goal of the runner?
   Runners have one goal in mind—the finish line.

5. Describe a time when you wanted to quit, but you kept your eyes on the Lord and pressed on? If you have already seen the rewards from this endurance, list them.
   Answers will vary.

6. What in your life may be restricting you from the greatest efficiency in serving the Lord? What steps should you take to lay aside these "weights"?
   Answers will vary.

7. How does patience relate to racing? What are the benefits of patience for the Christian runner?
Patience in a race is the ability to endure until the finish line. Patience enables a runner to win, and it helps spiritual runners to mature in their walk with the Lord and receive God's blessings in trials.

8. Have you ever made a commitment to finish your race strong to the glory of God? If not, make one today. What promises can you claim to help you remain faithful until the finish line?
Answers will vary.

Memory Verse

Philippians 3:14

14 I press toward the mark for the prize of the high calling of God in Christ Jesus.

LESSON SIX

A Sheep of Christ's Flock

Text

PSALM 95:7

7 *For he is our God; and we are the people of his pasture, and the sheep of his hand...*

PSALM 100:3

3 *Know ye that the LORD he is God: it is he that hath made us, and not we ourselves; we are his people, and the sheep of his pasture.*

Overview

The Bible frequently mentions sheep and shepherds, and Christ has lovingly claimed us as the sheep of His pasture. This lesson examines some Bible principles for how we, as sheep, should respond to the Good Shepherd.

Lesson Theme

As God's sheep, we need to hear His voice, follow His leading, and remain in His care.

Lesson Objectives

At the conclusion of the lesson, each student should:

1. Commit to reading and meditating on God's Word regularly.

2. Consecrate themselves to faithfully follow the Shepherd's leading.
3. Be fully convinced of God's trustworthiness to keep His promises and care for them.

Teaching Outline

Introduction

I. Hear the Shepherd's Voice—Allegiance
   A. Constantly feed.
   B. Submit to the Shepherd's control.

II. Follow the Shepherd's Lead—Action
   A. Keep moving, or become stagnant.
   B. Do not follow the crowd.

III. Remain in the Shepherd's Care—Abiding
   A. Depend on His protection.
   B. Depend on His promises.

Conclusion

LESSON SIX

A Sheep of Christ's Flock

Text

PSALM 95:7

7 *For he is our God; and we are the people of his pasture, and the sheep of his hand…*

PSALM 100:3

3 *Know ye that the LORD he is God: it is he that hath made us, and not we ourselves; we are his people, and the sheep of his pasture.*

Introduction

The Bible frequently mentions sheep and shepherds. A great deal of the Middle East is desert land, where it is not always possible to grow large amounts of crops. In Bible times, when irrigation was not as technologically advanced as it is today, many people raised animals rather than crops. Flocks were so relevant to the economy that a man's wealth could be measured by the size of his flocks.

If a man was wealthy enough to have more flocks than he and his sons could care for, he hired shepherds to care for the flocks. Obviously, the character and skill of these shepherds was of utmost importance to the owner of the flock. It was essential that these shepherds be capable and trustworthy men.

The Good Shepherd Himself cares for us, so we need not fear any harm coming to us through His ignorance or negligence. Let's examine some Bible principles for how we, as sheep, should respond to the Good Shepherd.

I. Hear the Shepherd's Voice —Allegiance

Sheep need to listen to the shepherd's voice. The shepherd's primary responsibility is to keep his sheep safe, so it is imperative that the sheep listen to and obey the shepherd.

Illustration

Those of us who have children know firsthand how important it is that our children learn to listen to us early. Their obedience could constitute a matter of life or death. If your small child wandered near a busy street and you were too far away to reach him, you would want him to be obedient to your shouted "STOP" before it was too late!

In God's infinite wisdom, He sees dangers that we cannot see, and He instructs us to listen to Him that we may avoid these dangers. Just as sheep need to listen to their shepherd, we need to listen to our Lord and discern His voice.

A. *Constantly feed.*

Sheep are almost constantly either eating or chewing their cud. Sheep are "ruminants" just like cattle, which means they have a digestive process that involves their food passing through different chambers of the stomach and periodically being brought back up so that they can chew it some more.

This behavior of sheep is such a good picture of the relationship we are to have with the Word of God. The Word of God is represented as something that we ingest into our hearts and minds, in much the same way as we take food into our stomachs.

Job 23:12
12 *Neither have I gone back from the commandment of his lips; I have esteemed the words of his mouth more than my necessary food.*

Psalm 34:8
8 *O taste and see that the Lord is good: blessed is the man that trusteth in him.*

Psalm 119:103
103 *How sweet are thy words unto my taste! yea, sweeter than honey to my mouth!*

We need to feast our souls and our spirits on the Word of God. As the physical body will deteriorate from lack of food, our spiritual lives will wither if we are not consuming God's Word. Being faithful to church and listening to the teaching and preaching of the Word, as well as maintaining a strong devotional life of your own, is imperative to your Christian life.

Paul explained to the Corinthian believers that he needed to teach them the basics of the Word of God, because they were not yet ready for its deeper teachings.

1 Corinthians 3:2

2 *I have fed you with milk, and not with meat: for hitherto ye were not able to bear it, neither yet now are ye able.*

The writer of Hebrews conveyed a similar thought.

Hebrews 5:12–14

12 *For when for the time ye ought to be teachers, ye have need that one teach you again which be the first principles of the oracles of God; and are become such as have need of milk, and not of strong meat.*

13 *For every one that useth milk is unskilful in the word of righteousness: for he is a babe.*

14 *But strong meat belongeth to them that are of full age, even those who by reason of use have their senses exercised to discern both good and evil.*

The Hebrews had not yet grown beyond the "baby" stage in their Christian life. They still required milk or the rudiments of God's Word, and their palate could not handle the deeper or stronger meat.

Let's think about a sheep as he ruminates on his cud. Notice the thoughtful look on his face as he chews! He doesn't just gulp it down as fast as he can and quickly bring up more cud; he gets every bit of nourishment he possibly can from each mouthful!

We "ruminate" on God's Word when we meditate on it. Simply reading the Bible will not give you enough

TEACHING TIP

Ask for a show of hands of how many students ate breakfast that morning (or whatever the most recent meal would have been). Ask how many ate something at some point the day before. Then ask them not to lift their hands for your final question: How many read their Bibles as recently as they ate?

God's Word is just as necessary to our spiritual health as food is to our physical health. Because our spiritual nourishment is even more important than our physical nourishment, we need to place spending time in God's Word even higher on our priority list than eating lunch!

spiritual nourishment. Think about it; consider it carefully; ponder it; "chew on it," and get all you can from each passage.

Would you like to be a successful Christian? God told Joshua how to achieve success.

Joshua 1:8

8 *This book of the law shall not depart out of thy mouth; but thou shalt meditate therein day and night, that thou mayest observe to do according to all that is written therein: for then thou shalt make thy way prosperous, and then thou shalt have good success.*

Would you like your life to be blessed by God? Psalm 1 tells us how it is done.

Psalm 1:1–2

1 *Blessed is the man that walketh not in the counsel of the ungodly, nor standeth in the way of sinners, nor sitteth in the seat of the scornful.*

2 *But his delight is in the law of the LORD; and in his law doth he meditate day and night.*

The longest chapter in the Bible, Psalm 119, centers on the psalmist's relationship with the Word of God. Five times in this chapter, meditation is mentioned.

PSALM 119:15, 23, 48, 78, 148
15 *I will meditate in thy precepts, and have respect unto thy ways.*
23 *Princes also did sit and speak against me: but thy servant did meditate in thy statutes.*
48 *My hands also will I lift up unto thy commandments, which I have loved; and I will meditate in thy statutes.*
78 *Let the proud be ashamed; for they dealt perversely with me without a cause: but I will meditate in thy precepts.*
148 *Mine eyes prevent the night watches, that I might meditate in thy word.*

Paul advised Timothy to engage in concentrated meditation on God's principles.

1 TIMOTHY 4:15
15 *Meditate upon these things; give thyself wholly to them; that thy profiting may appear to all.*

Develop the skill of listening to the voice of your Heavenly Shepherd by reading His Word and meditating on it.

B. Submit to the Shepherd's control.

The closer the sheep are to the shepherd, the safer the sheep will be. In fact, the word *shepherd* comes from the words "sheep" and "herd." It is the shepherd's job not only to protect and provide for the sheep, but he is also to control them or "herd" them. He needs to lead them to the best pastures and clean water. The sheep must submit to and follow the shepherd's leading.

As God's sheep, we, too, must submit to the control of our Shepherd. He knows best; we need to follow Him. Some of our best loved hymns address this submission.

> Trust and obey, for there's no other way
> To be happy in Jesus, but to trust and obey.
> —John H. Sammis

> Where He leads me I will follow,
> Where He leads me I will follow,
> Where He leads me I will follow;
> I'll go with Him, with Him, all the way.
> —Earnest W. Blandy

> He leadeth me, O blessèd thought!
> O words with heav'nly comfort fraught!
> Whate'er I do, where'er I be,
> Still 'tis God's hand that leadeth me.
> —Joseph H. Gilmore

The psalmists, too, expressed their need for God's leading in their lives.

Psalm 139:23–24

23 Search me, O God, and know my heart: try me, and know my thoughts:
24 And see if there be any wicked way in me, and lead me in the way everlasting.

Psalm 5:8

8 Lead me, O Lord, in thy righteousness because of mine enemies; make thy way straight before my face.

Psalm 32:8

8 I will instruct thee and teach thee in the way which thou shalt go: I will guide thee with mine eye.

If we will listen, God will speak; if we will follow, He will lead.

Sheep are safer by staying with the rest of the flock. They are especially susceptible to attack when they are separated from the flock. Predators watch for the sheep that separate themselves from the others, and many times that sheep becomes a predator's easy dinner.

Peter warns of the predator who stalks us.

1 Peter 5:8

8 Be sober, be vigilant; because your adversary the devil, as a roaring lion, walketh about, seeking whom he may devour:

The devil is our sworn enemy. He is out to devour every one of us—ruin our lives and take us away from the Lord. If we allow ourselves to become separated from God's people, we will become a much easier target for Satan. Paul warned the Ephesian elders about this.

Acts 20:29

29 For I know this, that after my departing shall grievous wolves enter in among you, not sparing the flock.

We must remain connected to our local church—faithful to its services and accountable to its members.

Hebrews 10:25

25 Not forsaking the assembling of ourselves together, as the manner of some is; but exhorting one another: and so much the more, as ye see the day approaching.

Give your Shepherd your complete allegiance by listening to His voice and following His control.

II. Follow the Shepherd's Lead—Action

We must learn to hear the Shepherd's voice—then we need to follow His lead. Let me share with you a couple of principles involved in following the Lord our Shepherd.

A. Keep moving, or become stagnant.

When sheep graze, they eat the grass all the way down to the roots, which can quickly kill the grass and destroy the land. To prevent overgrazing, shepherds must constantly move their sheep to fresh pasture.

Illustration

Perhaps you played the game "Cowboys and Indians" when you were young, thinking you were reenacting the days of the Old West. In actuality, the cowboys and Indians fought much less with each other than they did with others. Most of the time, the Indians were fighting either the soldiers (as in Custer's last stand), the railroad men, or the miners. As for the cowboys, when they weren't fighting each other over a card game in a saloon, they often fought with the sheep ranchers in what was known as "range wars."

Because of sheep's grazing methods, land grazed by sheep became useless for cattle. And because of sheep's need to continually move to new pasture, the cowboys felt sheep ranchers were continually taking the open ranges they needed for their cattle. Many range wars were quite violent.

We, too, must continually be on the move, or we will stagnate. Peter reminds us that we need constant growth.

2 Peter 3:18

18 But grow in grace, and in the knowledge of our Lord and Saviour Jesus Christ. To him be glory both now and for ever. Amen.

Paul maintained a consistent momentum as he moved forward for the Lord.

Philippians 3:14

14 I press toward the mark for the prize of the high calling of God in Christ Jesus.

This is one reason why each church must continually work to advance the cause of Christ. Each pastor should always look and plan ahead to keep the ministry moving forward for the Lord. If we don't move forward, we become stagnant and soon start to move backward.

B. Do not follow the crowd.

Sheep have a strong instinct to follow other sheep in the flock. When one sheep decides to go somewhere, the rest of the flock usually follows, even if doing so brings harm. Even from birth, lambs are conditioned to follow the older members of the flock.

Illustration

A *USA Today* article reported a mass suicide of sheep in Turkey. While the shepherds briefly left the flock, one sheep jumped off a cliff. When the shepherds returned, they were unable to stop the almost 1,500 remaining sheep from following. Four hundred fifty sheep were killed because they followed the crowd. [Source: *USA Today* article, July 8, 2005, http://www.usatoday.com/news/offbeat/2005–07–08-sheep-suicide_x.htm]

Does this principle cautioning us not to follow the wrong crowd contradict the earlier statements in this lesson encouraging God's people to stay close to one another? No. Sheep need the flock for protection, but they must listen to the shepherd for wise direction.

Each of us is individually accountable to God.

Romans 14:12

12 *So then every one of us shall give account of himself to God.*

2 Corinthians 5:10

10 *For we must all appear before the judgment seat of Christ; that every one may receive the things done in his body, according to that he hath done, whether it be good or bad.*

If we choose to follow the crowd in a direction that leads away from God, we are responsible for the consequences of our own decisions. We can follow godly people only as long as they are following Christ.

1 Corinthians 11:1

1 *Be ye followers of me, even as I also am of Christ.*

God specifically commanded the Israelites to refuse to follow those who were making wrong choices.

Exodus 23:2

2 *Thou shalt not follow a multitude to do evil; neither shalt thou speak in a cause to decline after many to wrest judgment:*

Scriptural examples of those who followed the crowd to their own destruction are numerous, especially during Israel's journey to the Promised Land. Frequently, complaining and murmuring would be heard in the camp, and soon the whole crowd would rise up against Moses. In the case of Korah's rebellion (Numbers 16), thousands of people died because they followed the crowd in rebellion against God. When the Israelites reached the Promised Land, they believed the report of the ten faithless spies who convinced them that they could not take the Promised Land rather than listening to Joshua and Caleb's faithful report. They paid dearly for this decision for the next forty years (Numbers 13–14).

The crowd is fickle and easily swayed. When Jesus rode into Jerusalem, the multitudes all hailed Him, "*Hosanna to the Son of David: Blessed is he that cometh in the name of the Lord; Hosanna in the highest*" (Matthew 21:9). Just a few days later, those same multitudes were calling out, "*Crucify him, crucify him*" (Luke 23:21).

People who follow the crowd without thinking for themselves often find themselves reaping unforeseen consequences. We must listen for our Shepherd's voice and be obedient to follow His direction.

III. Remain in the Shepherd's Care —Abiding

Wealthy sheep owners who had more flocks than they could care for alone were very careful in their selection of the shepherds they hired because a sheep's welfare is entirely dependent on the shepherd. Their sheep were not just pets; they literally were the livelihood of the family. They were valuable animals which required diligent care of the shepherd.

We, too, are valuable to God. He calls us the sheep of His pasture (Psalm 100:3), and He inspired David to write that the

Lord was his shepherd (Psalm 23:1). The entire twenty-third Psalm details the tender care of the Lord for His people.

A. *Depend on His protection.*

Many animals, even domestic animals, can defend themselves effectively if necessary. But sheep cannot defend themselves. All but the toughest rams would be utterly helpless against any predator. (Remember that David killed both a lion and a bear that had attacked his flock. He took the lamb right out of the bear's mouth. Without David's protection, there would have been no hope for the sheep.)

We already identified our enemy—Satan. Scripture commands us to resist him.

1 Peter 5:8–9

8 Be sober, be vigilant; because your adversary the devil, as a roaring lion, walketh about, seeking whom he may devour:

9 Whom resist stedfast in the faith, knowing that the same afflictions are accomplished in your brethren that are in the world.

James 4:7

7 Submit yourselves therefore to God. Resist the devil, and he will flee from you.

Yet we cannot defeat Satan apart from the Lord. Jesus withstood the temptations of Satan in the wilderness by quoting the Word of God (Matthew 4:1–11; Luke 4:1–13). Even the angels rely on the Lord when it comes to resisting the devil (Jude 9).

As the sheep depend on the protection of their shepherd, so we depend on the Lord.

Illustration

Many of us have had near-death experiences and have seen the Lord's miraculous intervention that spared our lives. There must be many more times that we have had near-death experiences and never even knew it because the Lord protected us before we ever noticed anything.

We often do not see God's continual hand of protection. Be conscious always of His presence.

TEACHING TIP

Relate an experience in your own life in which you saw God miraculously spare you from death to use with the illustration above.

God is always watching over you.

Psalm 121:4
4 *Behold, he that keepeth Israel shall neither slumber nor sleep.*

The God who keeps and watches over you never drops His attention. Nothing can happen to us that He does not either cause or permit, and in either case, His love is at work. We depend on God's protection.

Psalm 23:4
4 *Yea, though I walk through the valley of the shadow of death, I will fear no evil: for thou art with me; thy rod and thy staff they comfort me.*

We also depend on God's protection for our eternal future. Some struggle with the assurance of their salvation.

They think that through sinful living they could lose their eternal home. Once we've trusted Christ as our Saviour, however, our salvation is guarded by God.

John 10:27–29

27 *My sheep hear my voice, and I know them, and they follow me:*
28 *And I give unto them eternal life; and they shall never perish, neither shall any man pluck them out of my hand.*
29 *My Father, which gave them me, is greater than all; and no man is able to pluck them out of my Father's hand.*

We'll spend more time in this passage in our next lesson, but for now, be assured that your salvation is safe in God's hand.

B. Depend on His promises.

The outstanding characteristic of the shepherd is his reliability. The sheep depend on him to take them to fresh pastures, to lead them in the right direction, and to protect them from hazards. In everything, the sheep trust the shepherd.

Twice in John 10, Jesus assures us, "*I am the good shepherd*" (John 10:11, 14). The Good Shepherd will never let His sheep down. We can trust in the promises of our Good Shepherd.

Psalm 9:10

10 *And they that know thy name will put their trust in thee: for thou, Lord, hast not forsaken them that seek thee.*

We have the promise of His presence, now and forever.

Psalm 37:28

28 For the Lord loveth judgment, and forsaketh not his saints; they are preserved for ever: but the seed of the wicked shall be cut off.

Hebrews 13:5

5 Let your conversation be without covetousness; and be content with such things as ye have: for he hath said, I will never leave thee, nor forsake thee.

1 Corinthians 2:9

9 But as it is written, Eye hath not seen, nor ear heard, neither have entered into the heart of man, the things which God hath prepared for them that love him.

We have the promise of His peace.

John 14:27

27 Peace I leave with you, my peace I give unto you: not as the world giveth, give I unto you. Let not your heart be troubled, neither let it be afraid.

John 16:33

33 These things I have spoken unto you, that in me ye might have peace. In the world ye shall have tribulation: but be of good cheer; I have overcome the world.

Romans 5:1

1 Therefore being justified by faith, we have peace with God through our Lord Jesus Christ:

Philippians 4:6–7

6 Be careful for nothing; but in every thing by prayer and supplication with thanksgiving let your requests be made known unto God.

7 And the peace of God, which passeth all understanding, shall keep your hearts and minds through Christ Jesus.

We have the promise of His return.

John 14:1–3

1 Let not your heart be troubled: ye believe in God, believe also in me.
2 In my Father's house are many mansions: if it were not so, I would have told you. I go to prepare a place for you.
3 And if I go and prepare a place for you, I will come again, and receive you unto myself; that where I am, there ye may be also.

1 Thessalonians 4:13–18

13 But I would not have you to be ignorant, brethren, concerning them which are asleep, that ye sorrow not, even as others which have no hope.
14 For if we believe that Jesus died and rose again, even so them also which sleep in Jesus will God bring with him.
15 For this we say unto you by the word of the Lord, that we which are alive and remain unto the coming of the Lord shall not prevent them which are asleep.
16 For the Lord himself shall descend from heaven with a shout, with the voice of the archangel, and with the trump of God: and the dead in Christ shall rise first:
17 Then we which are alive and remain shall be caught up together with them in the clouds, to meet the Lord in the air: and so shall we ever be with the Lord.
18 Wherefore comfort one another with these words.

This is just a sampling of the "*exceeding great and precious promises*" God had given us (2 Peter 1:4). And these promises are backed by God's unfailing faithfulness. Our own past experiences also affirm God's reliability.

Joshua testified of God's unfailing promises at the end of his life.

Joshua 23:14

14 *And, behold, this day I am going the way of all the earth: and ye know in all your hearts and in all your souls, that not one thing hath failed of all the good things which the Lord your God spake concerning you; all are come to pass unto you, and not one thing hath failed thereof.*

You can trust your Shepherd, so rest in His care.

Conclusion

As God's sheep, we need to develop the skill of hearing our Shepherd's voice. This requires reading and meditating on God's Word.

After we hear God's voice, we need to obediently follow His leading. Sometimes we will be tempted to follow others down paths of disobedience. But these paths are paths of destruction. Our Shepherd's voice is the only one that can be unreservedly trusted.

We must constantly be alert for our lion-like enemy—Satan. He is ever on the prowl for opportunities to destroy our lives. Our Shepherd, however, provides protection through His Word. By reading and meditating upon God's Word, we can resist our enemy.

Our Shepherd is ever vigilant and is always available in our times of distress. He has provided us with His unfailing promises to encourage our hearts and strengthen our faith.

What a joy it is to belong to such a Shepherd!

Study Questions

1. What does the rumination process of sheep teach us about how we feed on God's Word?
   We must "ruminate" on God's Word by meditating on it. Simply reading the Bible does not provide enough spiritual nourishment. We must "chew on it" to get all we can from each passage.

2. Who is our predator, and what is one way we can be protected from him?
   Satan seeks to devour us as a lion would devour a sheep. Remaining close to God's people can provide protection. God's Word can also be used to resist him.

3. Does the principle cautioning us not to follow the wrong crowd contradict the principle of needing to stay close to God's people? Why or why not?
   The principles do not contradict. Sheep need the flock for protection, but they must listen to the shepherd for wise direction.

4. What is the outstanding characteristic of the shepherd? How does this relate to our ability to trust God?
   The outstanding characteristic of the shepherd is his reliability. Twice in John 10, Jesus assures us, "I am the good shepherd" (John 10:11, 14). The Good Shepherd will never let His sheep down.

5. Describe a time in your life when you sensed the Holy Spirit warning you of danger (perhaps through His Word, your pastor, or another godly Christian). Did you heed or ignore His warnings? What was the outcome?
   Answers will vary.

6. Are you as consistent and regular in digesting spiritual food (God's Word) as you are physical food? What changes can you make to give the spiritual food God provides the priority it deserves?
   Answers will vary.

7. Flocks of sheep must be regularly moved to new pastures. In what ways have you grown in the past three months?
   Answers will vary.

8. Do you have friends or acquaintances with whom you need to limit contact to avoid being drawn into temptation? List some.
   Answers will vary.

Memory Verses

Psalm 95:7

7 For he is our God; and we are the people of his pasture, and the sheep of his hand....

Psalm 100:3

3 Know ye that the Lord he is God: it is he that hath made us, and not we ourselves; we are his people, and the sheep of his pasture.

LESSON SEVEN

A Sheep in Christ's Care

Text

JOHN 10:2–18, 27

2 *But he that entereth in by the door is the shepherd of*
the sheep.
3 *To him the porter openeth; and the sheep hear his voice:*
and he calleth his own sheep by name, and leadeth them out.
4 *And when he putteth forth his own sheep, he goeth before*
them, and the sheep follow him: for they know his voice.
5 *And a stranger will they not follow, but will flee from him:*
for they know not the voice of strangers.
6 *This parable spake Jesus unto them: but they understood*
not what things they were which he spake unto them.
7 *Then said Jesus unto them again, Verily, verily, I say unto*
you, I am the door of the sheep.
8 *All that ever came before me are thieves and robbers: but*
the sheep did not hear them.
9 *I am the door: by me if any man enter in, he shall be saved,*
and shall go in and out, and find pasture.
10 *The thief cometh not, but for to steal, and to kill, and to*
destroy: I am come that they might have life, and that they
might have it more abundantly.
11 *I am the good shepherd: the good shepherd giveth his life*
for the sheep.
12 *But he that is an hireling, and not the shepherd, whose*
own the sheep are not, seeth the wolf coming, and leaveth the

sheep, and fleeth: and the wolf catcheth them, and scattereth the sheep.
13 *The hireling fleeth, because he is an hireling, and careth not for the sheep.*
14 *I am the good shepherd, and know my sheep, and am known of mine.*
15 *As the Father knoweth me, even so know I the Father: and I lay down my life for the sheep.*
16 *And other sheep I have, which are not of this fold: them also I must bring, and they shall hear my voice; and there shall be one fold, and one shepherd.*
17 *Therefore doth my Father love me, because I lay down my life, that I might take it again.*
18 *No man taketh it from me, but I lay it down of myself. I have power to lay it down, and I have power to take it again. This commandment have I received of my Father.*
27 *My sheep hear my voice, and I know them, and they follow me:*

Overview

Sheep have a special relationship with their shepherd that is characterized by dependence (on the part of the sheep) and dependability (on the part of the shepherd). This is a picture of the relationship our Good Shepherd wants to have with us.

Lesson Theme

Our Good Shepherd invites us to come to Him for every need we have. Coming from any other source, this promise would be unbelievable, but coming from God Himself, this promise is one that we know will be fulfilled each and every day.

To properly nurture our relationship with our Shepherd, we must listen to His voice and follow Him in loving obedience. By doing so, we can more accurately portray His love to others.

Lesson Objectives

At the conclusion of the lesson, each student should:

1. Know that Jesus Christ is approachable and that His arms are open to all who come.
2. Understand their need as sheep to hear and obey the Shepherd's voice.
3. Commit to demonstrating God's love and grace by their attitude of love and service for others.

Teaching Outline

Introduction

I. Coming to the Shepherd
   A. Come for salvation.
   B. Come for strength.

II. Following the Shepherd
   A. Hear His voice.
   B. Obey His commands.

III. Loving the Shepherd
   A. We love Him by obeying.
   B. We love Him by loving others.

Conclusion

LESSON SEVEN

A Sheep in Christ's Care

Text

JOHN 10:2–18, 27

2 *But he that entereth in by the door is the shepherd of the sheep.*

3 *To him the porter openeth; and the sheep hear his voice: and he calleth his own sheep by name, and leadeth them out.*

4 *And when he putteth forth his own sheep, he goeth before them, and the sheep follow him: for they know his voice.*

5 *And a stranger will they not follow, but will flee from him: for they know not the voice of strangers.*

6 *This parable spake Jesus unto them: but they understood not what things they were which he spake unto them.*

7 *Then said Jesus unto them again, Verily, verily, I say unto you, I am the door of the sheep.*

8 *All that ever came before me are thieves and robbers: but the sheep did not hear them.*

9 I am the door: by me if any man enter in, he shall be saved, and shall go in and out, and find pasture.
10 The thief cometh not, but for to steal, and to kill, and to destroy: I am come that they might have life, and that they might have it more abundantly.
11 I am the good shepherd: the good shepherd giveth his life for the sheep.
12 But he that is an hireling, and not the shepherd, whose own the sheep are not, seeth the wolf coming, and leaveth the sheep, and fleeth: and the wolf catcheth them, and scattereth the sheep.
13 The hireling fleeth, because he is an hireling, and careth not for the sheep.
14 I am the good shepherd, and know my sheep, and am known of mine.
15 As the Father knoweth me, even so know I the Father: and I lay down my life for the sheep.
16 And other sheep I have, which are not of this fold: them also I must bring, and they shall hear my voice; and there shall be one fold, and one shepherd.
17 Therefore doth my Father love me, because I lay down my life, that I might take it again.
18 No man taketh it from me, but I lay it down of myself. I have power to lay it down, and I have power to take it again. This commandment have I received of my Father.
27 My sheep hear my voice, and I know them, and they follow me:

Introduction

Sheep have a special relationship with their shepherd that is characterized by dependence (on the part of the sheep) and dependability (on the part of the shepherd). This is a picture of the relationship our Good Shepherd wants to have with us. In our last lesson, we studied some of the characteristics of sheep, and in this lesson we will focus on the sheep's relationship to the shepherd.

Sheep are valuable to their shepherd. Jesus used an illustration of one lost sheep out of a flock of one hundred to show how precious each individual person is to God.

Matthew 18:11–14

11 *For the Son of man is come to save that which was lost.*
12 *How think ye? if a man have an hundred sheep, and one of them be gone astray, doth he not leave the ninety and nine, and goeth into the mountains, and seeketh that which is gone astray?*
13 *And if so be that he find it, verily I say unto you, he rejoiceth more of that sheep, than of the ninety and nine which went not astray.*
14 *Even so it is not the will of your Father which is in heaven, that one of these little ones should perish.*

Let's consider our relationship to our Lord, "*that great shepherd of the sheep*" (Hebrews 13:20).

I. Coming to the Shepherd

We tend to avoid certain types of people. For example, we dread spending time with those who are critical, complaining, or harsh. On the other hand, there are people whose company we enjoy very much. We feel drawn to those who encourage and inspire, to those who are thoughtful and giving, to those who are joyful and fun.

Jesus drew people nearly everywhere He went. They came to Him for healing of illnesses and afflictions; they came when they needed spiritual guidance; they came on behalf of others who needed help; and they came because they wanted to hear His teaching. Jesus was approachable.

No one who came to Jesus with a sincere and willing heart was turned away. Whatever the need, Jesus was able and willing to meet that need. It was as simple as the story of the leper who came to Jesus and said, "*Lord, if thou wilt, thou canst make me clean.*" Jesus simply answered, "*I will: be thou clean.*" He touched the leprous man, "*And immediately the leprosy departed from him*" (Luke 5:12–13).

Jesus' arms are still open as the loving Shepherd who is always there to meet the needs of His sheep. Come to the Shepherd.

A. Come for salvation.

The greatest need each person faces is the need for salvation, and this salvation can only be found in Jesus Christ.

John 10:7, 9

7 *Then said Jesus unto them again, Verily, verily, I say unto you, I am the door of the sheep.*

9 *I am the door: by me if any man enter in, he shall be saved, and shall go in and out, and find pasture.*

Jesus did not say, "I am *a* door" or "I am *one of* the doors." He said, "I am *the* door."

Illustration

Some rooms, like our church auditorium, have several doors, several ways in and out of the room. When it comes to salvation, however, there is only *one* way. We can only enter into the presence of God through the Lord Jesus Christ.

John 14:6

6 *Jesus saith unto him, I am the way, the truth, and the life: no man cometh unto the Father, but by me.*

Acts 4:12

12 *Neither is there salvation in any other: for there is none other name under heaven given among men, whereby we must be saved.*

1 John 5:11–12

11 *And this is the record, that God hath given to us eternal life, and this life is in his Son.*
12 *He that hath the Son hath life; and he that hath not the Son of God hath not life.*

Scripture is very clear that salvation comes only through the Lord Jesus Christ.

Titus 3:5

5 *Not by works of righteousness which we have done, but according to his mercy he saved us, by the washing of regeneration, and renewing of the Holy Ghost;*

As we mentioned in our last lesson, sheep are defenseless. When they are threatened, their only chance for protection is in their shepherd. In his presence they are safe from harm.

We can't find forgiveness from our sins by our own merit. Only when we come to Jesus and put our trust in the blood He shed for our sins, can we find forgiveness and salvation from God.

B. Come for strength.

Just as sheep are dependent on their shepherd for everything, so we are dependent on Christ. Using another analogy to explain our relationship with Christ, Jesus stated our dependence on Him.

JOHN 15:5

5 *I am the vine, ye are the branches: He that abideth in me, and I in him, the same bringeth forth much fruit: for* ***without me ye can do nothing.***

The Apostle Paul thought he was a strong man before he met Christ.

PHILIPPIANS 3:4–6

4 *Though I might also have confidence in the flesh. If any other man thinketh that he hath whereof he might trust in the flesh, I more:*
5 *Circumcised the eighth day, of the stock of Israel, of the tribe of Benjamin, an Hebrew of the Hebrews; as touching the law, a Pharisee;*
6 *Concerning zeal, persecuting the church; touching the righteousness which is in the law, blameless.*

As a religious unbeliever, Paul thought he had everything in place. After he became a Christian, God allowed a specific weakness in his life so he would continually rely on the Lord's strength.

2 CORINTHIANS 12:7–10

7 *And lest I should be exalted above measure through the abundance of the revelations, there was given to me a thorn in the flesh, the messenger of Satan to buffet me, lest I should be exalted above measure.*
8 *For this thing I besought the Lord thrice, that it might depart from me.*
9 *And he said unto me, My grace is sufficient for thee: for my strength is made perfect in weakness. Most gladly*

therefore will I rather glory in my infirmities, that the power of Christ may rest upon me.
10 *Therefore I take pleasure in infirmities, in reproaches, in necessities, in persecutions, in distresses for Christ's sake: for when I am weak, then am I strong.*

If the Apostle Paul needed to come to the Lord for strength, surely we do! Isaiah 40:28–31 is a challenge to all of us, to find strength in the Lord.

Isaiah 40:28–31

28 *Hast thou not known? hast thou not heard, that the everlasting God, the Lord, the Creator of the ends of the earth, fainteth not, neither is weary? there is no searching of his understanding.*
29 *He giveth power to the faint; and to them that have no might he increaseth strength.*
30 *Even the youths shall faint and be weary, and the young men shall utterly fall:*
31 *But they that wait upon the Lord shall renew their strength; they shall mount up with wings as eagles; they shall run, and not be weary; and they shall walk, and not faint.*

Jesus Himself needed special strength as He neared Calvary. During His time of prayer in the garden, He received strength from above when He needed it.

Luke 22:41–43

41 *And he was withdrawn from them about a stone's cast, and kneeled down, and prayed,*
42 *Saying, Father, if thou be willing, remove this cup from me: nevertheless not my will, but thine, be done.*
43 *And there appeared an angel unto him from heaven, strengthening him.*

Our Shepherd invites us personally to come to Him for strength.

Matthew 11:28–30

28 *Come unto me, all ye that labour and are heavy laden, and I will give you rest.*
29 *Take my yoke upon you, and learn of me; for I am meek and lowly in heart: and ye shall find rest unto your souls.*
30 *For my yoke is easy, and my burden is light.*

The sheep needs its shepherd, and we need the Lord. How precious it is that Jesus invites us to come to Him, first for salvation and *then* for strength. Run to His open arms.

II. Following the Shepherd

Once we come to our Shepherd, we need to follow Him. Because He is the Creator and Owner of both the sheep and the pasture, we belong to Him.

Psalm 100:3

3 *Know ye that the Lord he is God: it is he that hath made us, and not we ourselves; we are his people, and the sheep of his pasture.*

With the heart of a true Shepherd, God delights in guiding us through life.

Psalm 78:52

52 *But made his own people to go forth like sheep, and guided them in the wilderness like a flock.*

A. Hear His voice.

A sheep is drawn to the shepherd's voice. The sheep's ability to hear and recognize the shepherd's voice provides access to the shepherd's guidance.

Our key verses reveal that a sheep can distinguish its shepherd's voice from a stranger's voice. It flees from the stranger and follows the shepherd. Many voices in the world today consistently clamor for our attention. We have no shortage of advice and opinions. If you're having trouble with a particular decision in your life, you can seek guidance from many different places—some places, however, are better than others.

Illustration

If your car is making a noise you are sure it wasn't built to make, you can consult thousands of websites for help, or you can go to a repair shop and get the opinion of a qualified mechanic. (Or you could just turn the radio up louder so that you won't hear the noise anymore!)

Some counsel leads you in the right direction, and some leads you in the wrong direction. Even well-meaning friends can give poor guidance. The only counsel that is guaranteed to work is God's counsel. But how can we distinguish our Shepherd's voice from all of the voices that call to us?

TEACHING TIP

Ask your students to share some stories about how well-meaning counsel they received from someone they trusted ended in troublesome or humorous consequences.

Hearing God's voice begins with a willing heart. Just as the shepherd does not put his sheep on a leash to lead them, our Shepherd has allowed us a choice—He does not force us to follow Him. Are you willing to follow as He leads?

We must listen carefully for God's voice, for He does not shout; the loudest voice we hear is not necessarily God's voice. The prophet Elijah experienced the gentleness of God's voice. During a great trial in his life, he had a special visit from God while he was alone in a cave in Mount Horeb.

1 Kings 19:11–12
11 *And he said, Go forth, and stand upon the mount before the Lord. And, behold, the Lord passed by, and a great and strong wind rent the mountains, and brake in pieces the rocks before the Lord; but the Lord was not in the wind: and after the wind an earthquake; but the Lord was not in the earthquake:*
12 *And after the earthquake a fire; but the Lord was not in the fire: and after the fire a still small voice.*

The Lord did not speak through the wind or the earthquake or the fire; He spoke in a still small voice. When Elijah heard that voice, He came out of the cave to speak with God. Are you listening for that still, small voice?

The voice of God *always* lines up with the Word of God. God does guide us individually, but He will *never* guide us contrary to the commands and principles He has already revealed in His Word. When you need God's guidance and direction for a particular area, start by studying all that God's Word teaches on that subject. Listen carefully in church; God will speak to your personal need through the messages from His Word. Ask God to give you the direction you need, and seek counsel from godly people who know God's Word. One of the key ways to learn to discern the Shepherd's voice is by spending quality time reading His Word every day.

B. Obey His commands.

Obedience to the shepherd's commands may be a matter of life or death for the sheep. The shepherd can see dangers that the sheep cannot see, and he guides them in the right direction. Even so, God sees what we cannot see and knows the best direction for our lives.

Isaiah 55:8–9

8 *For my thoughts are not your thoughts, neither are your ways my ways, saith the Lord.*
9 *For as the heavens are higher than the earth, so are my ways higher than your ways, and my thoughts than your thoughts.*

Our Shepherd knows what is best for us, and we ought to submit ourselves in obedience to Him. Jesus explained that we cannot say we are following the Lord if we do not obey Him.

Luke 6:46

46 *And why call ye me, Lord, Lord, and do not the things which I say?*

The Apostle John puts the matter very plainly.

1 John 1:6–7

6 *If we say that we have fellowship with him, and walk in darkness, we lie, and do not the truth:*

7 *But if we walk in the light, as he is in the light, we have fellowship one with another, and the blood of Jesus Christ his Son cleanseth us from all sin.*

As it has often been said, "Your talk talks, and your walk talks. But your walk talks louder than your talk talks." We can *say* we are following the Lord, but our actions are the real test of our obedience.

John 14:15

15 *If ye love me, keep my commandments.*

James gives an illustration of the folly of simply hearing God's Word, but neglecting to heed it. He compares this neglect to a man who looks in the mirror, sees changes he needs to make in his appearance, but turns away without making the needed changes.

James 1:22–25

22 *But be ye doers of the word, and not hearers only, deceiving your own selves.*

23 *For if any be a hearer of the word, and not a doer, he is like unto a man beholding his natural face in a glass:*

24 *For he beholdeth himself, and goeth his way, and straightway forgetteth what manner of man he was.*

25 *But whoso looketh into the perfect law of liberty, and continueth therein, he being not a forgetful hearer, but a doer of the work, this man shall be blessed in his deed.*

It is not enough just to know what the Bible says; we need to be changed by God's truths. How foolish it would be to come to the Shepherd, to listen for His voice, and then to refuse to follow His leading.

III. Loving the Shepherd

Behind each of God's commands is a love that we cannot even begin to comprehend. Simply stated, "*God is love*" (1 John 4:8). And God has made us to respond to His love. "We *love him, because he first loved us*" (1 John 4:19).

A lawyer once came to Jesus and asked him to name the greatest commandment.

Matthew 22:35–38
35 *Then one of them, which was a lawyer, asked him a question, tempting him, and saying,*
36 *Master, which is the great commandment in the law?*
37 *Jesus said unto him, Thou shalt love the Lord thy God with all thy heart, and with all thy soul, and with all thy mind.*
38 *This is the first and great commandment.*

If we indeed love the Lord with all of our hearts and all of our souls and all of our minds, we will have no problem listening to His voice and following His commands. Our actions will freely declare our love for Him.

A. We love Him by obeying.

Our motive for obedience to Christ must be love.

Illustration

Most of us have experienced the strain of working for a boss or manager whom we do not particularly like or respect. We obey because we want to keep our jobs, but we sometimes struggle with resentment even as we obey.

Contrast that scenario with working for someone whom you genuinely like and respect. It makes a tremendous difference—the outward actions may be the same, but the attitude of love makes obedience much easier and even enjoyable.

Illustration

The practice of slavery was a great scourge in American history. There were some cases, however, where slaves were well-treated by their masters. Some of these slaves chose to stay and serve their former masters after they were granted their freedom. Before they were freed, they served because they *had* to. As they grew to know and develop a relationship with their masters, they served because they *wanted* to. In both cases, they served, but the attitude of love for the master made a wonderful difference in the heart of the servant. If we love our Lord, we will be happy to serve and obey Him.

Our obedience to God's Word is evidence of our love for God and even of our salvation.

1 John 2:5

5 *But whoso keepeth his word, in him verily is the love of God perfected: hereby know we that we are in him.*

B. *We love Him by loving others.*

Jesus said the greatest commandment is to love God, but the second commandment is to love others.

Matthew 22:39

39 *And the second is like unto it, Thou shalt love thy neighbour as thyself.*

Loving God and loving others cannot be separated. We show our love for God by loving others.

1 John 4:21

21 And this commandment have we from him, That he who loveth God love his brother also.

How easy it is to be so consumed by our own burdens and problems that we lose sight of the needs of others. God wants to open our eyes to the needs of those around us.

Illustration

No matter how difficult my problem is, I have found that I don't have to look very far to find someone who has it worse. When I focus on how I can meet others' needs and encourage them, I find that God often lifts my burden in the process!

How can we say that we have the love of God when we do not seek to meet the needs of those around us?

1 John 3:17

17 But whoso hath this world's good, and seeth his brother have need, and shutteth up his bowels of compassion from him, how dwelleth the love of God in him?

After Jesus' Resurrection, He challenged Peter to show his love for Christ. You will remember that Peter had denied Jesus three times and afterward repented with bitter tears. Jesus graciously and lovingly restored Peter to His fellowship and three times asked the question, "*Lovest thou me?*"

Peter did love Jesus and told Him so. Jesus gave Peter the opportunity and privilege of showing that love by serving others.

John 21:15–17
15 *So when they had dined, Jesus saith to Simon Peter, Simon, son of Jonas, lovest thou me more than these? He saith unto him, Yea, Lord; thou knowest that I love thee. He saith unto him, Feed my lambs.*
16 *He saith to him again the second time, Simon, son of Jonas, lovest thou me? He saith unto him, Yea, Lord; thou knowest that I love thee. He saith unto him, Feed my sheep.*
17 *He saith unto him the third time, Simon, son of Jonas, lovest thou me? Peter was grieved because he said unto him the third time, Lovest thou me? And he said unto him, Lord, thou knowest all things; thou knowest that I love thee. Jesus saith unto him, Feed my sheep.*

We could paraphrase: "Do you love Me, Peter? Then feed My sheep; love My people, and meet their needs." Do you love the Lord, Christian? Then demonstrate that love by loving others and living for others.

Conclusion

This Shepherd/sheep relationship begins with our coming to the Shepherd for salvation. Then, Jesus invites us to come to Him for every need we have, including our need for daily strength. Coming from any other source, this promise would be unbelievable, but coming from God Himself, this is a promise we know will be fulfilled each and every day.

God's love is beyond our comprehension. To properly nurture our relationship with our Shepherd, we must listen to His voice and follow Him in loving obedience. By doing so, we can more accurately portray His love to others.

Study Questions

1. As we come to the Shepherd, what is the first and greatest need in our spiritual life?
   Our greatest need is salvation which can only be found in Jesus Christ.

2. What are two characteristics of the special relationship sheep have with their shepherd?
   Two characteristics of the relationship between shepherd and sheep are dependence and dependability.

3. What should be our motive for obeying Christ?
   The motive for obeying Christ should be love.

4. How do we demonstrate God's love for us?
   We demonstrate God's love for us by loving others (see illustration of Peter and Christ—"Lovest thou me?").

5. Has there been a specific time when you have seen the protection of the Good Shepherd in the midst of difficulties in your life? How were you able to see His dependability and/or sense His strength?
   Answers will vary.

6. Describe a situation in which you knew what the Lord was telling you to do, but you chose instead to go your own way. In what ways did you find that this stubbornness removed you from the shelter of the Shepherd's protection? Ask the Lord to reveal any current areas of your life which you have not submitted to His direction.
   Answers will vary.

7. Sheep need to learn to listen attentively to the voice of the Shepherd. What are some ways you can increase your ability to hear and recognize the Shepherd's voice?
Answers will vary but may include the following: praying before devotions or a church service for an open and submissive heart, being quick to respond when He speaks, spending time alone with Him in quiet so other voices are tuned out.

8. When was the last time you physically demonstrated God's love by helping someone in need? Did you find that your own love for God increased? Explain.
Answers will vary.

Memory Verse

John 10:9

9 I am the door: by me if any man enter in, he shall be saved, and shall go in and out, and find pasture.

LESSON EIGHT

A Disciple of Christ

Text

JOHN 8:31

31 *Then said Jesus to those Jews which believed on him, If ye continue in my word, then are ye my disciples indeed.*

JOHN 13:35

35 *By this shall all men know that ye are my disciples, if ye have love one to another.*

Overview

A disciple is a pupil—one who learns from another's teachings. As Christians, we are disciples of Christ and have an important relationship with the Master Teacher.

Lesson Theme

As disciples, we must be ready to fulfill our three-fold purpose: to answer the call to be a follower of Jesus Christ, to accept criticism joyfully, and to relay the Good News to others.

Lesson Objectives

At the conclusion of the lesson, each student should:

1. Understand the relationship that Christ desires to have with His disciples.

2. Know that criticism for Christ's sake is part of what makes us distinctive followers of Christ.
3. Execute the disciple's prime responsibility to go and tell the world about the death, burial, and resurrection of Jesus Christ.

Teaching Outline

Introduction

I. A Disciple Is Called
   A. To be with Him
   B. To be like Him

II. A Disciple Is Criticized
   A. Corporately
   B. Individually

III. A Disciple Is Commissioned
   A. To learn
   B. To tell

Conclusion

LESSON EIGHT

A Disciple of Christ

Text

John 8:31

31 *Then said Jesus to those Jews which believed on him, If ye continue in my word, then are ye my disciples indeed.*

John 13:35

35 *By this shall all men know that ye are my disciples, if ye have love one to another.*

Introduction

The word *disciple* simply means "learner" or "pupil." In this lesson we will focus on the relationship between the Master Teacher, the Lord Jesus Christ, and us as His pupils.

Lazarus' sisters, Mary and Martha, demonstrate two different types of disciples. When Jesus visited in their home, Martha bustled around in service, while Mary simply sat at

Jesus' feet. When Martha complained of Mary's lack of service, Jesus gently rebuked Martha's lack of listening: "*Martha, thou art careful and troubled about many things: But one thing is needful: and Mary hath chosen that good part, which shall not be taken away from her*" (Luke 10:41–42).

Taking time to simply sit at the feet of Jesus and listen as He speaks is the attitude of a disciple. Jesus invites us all, "*Come unto me…and learn of me…*" (Matthew 11:28–29). The invitation is open—we need to respond. The Lord is eager to teach—we need to be eager to learn.

I. A Disciple Is Called

Jesus had many disciples, but He had twelve whom He specifically called to Him and specially chose to teach and train (Luke 6:13–16). The calling these twelve received applies to us today and involves two parts.

A. To be with Him

Matthew 4:18–22

18 *And Jesus, walking by the sea of Galilee, saw two brethren, Simon called Peter, and Andrew his brother, casting a net into the sea: for they were fishers.*

19 *And he saith unto them, Follow me, and I will make you fishers of men.*

20 *And they straightway left their nets, and followed him.*

21 *And going on from thence, he saw other two brethren, James the son of Zebedee, and John his brother, in a ship with Zebedee their father, mending their nets; and he called them.*

22 *And they immediately left the ship and their father, and followed him.*

Answering Christ's call to be a disciple meant witnessing firsthand His working miracles and meeting the needs of those whom no one else could help. They saw Him heal the sick and afflicted, feed the multitudes, calm the raging sea, and restore the dead to life. They heard His words of wisdom, comfort, and rebuke. In those days, the disciples stayed with Jesus and followed Him wherever He went. Today the Lord, through the person of the Holy Spirit, indwells all Christian believers and is present with us at all times.

Romans 8:9, 11
9 *But ye are not in the flesh, but in the Spirit, if so be that*
the Spirit of God ***dwell in you.*** *Now if any man have not*
the Spirit of Christ, he is none of his.
11 *But if the Spirit of him that raised up Jesus from the*
dead ***dwell in you,*** *he that raised up Christ from the dead*
shall also quicken your mortal bodies by his Spirit that
dwelleth in you.

The Holy Spirit indwells every person who has trusted Christ as their Saviour. He is always with us, and He desires that we would always be aware of His presence. We are called to be with Him, yet sometimes we try to compartmentalize our lives and keep the Lord out of some areas. We need to remain cognizant of His presence in our lives.

Many Old Testament saints provided an example of living in the presence of the Lord. Enoch "*walked with God*" (Genesis 5:22, 24). Noah "*walked with God*" (Genesis 6:9). Several Old Testament kings "*did that which was right in the sight of the Lord*" (2 Kings 18:3, 22:2; 2 Chronicles 24:2).

Living in the presence of the Lord means that sometimes hardships will come. In Matthew 26, we read about the Last Supper, where Jesus said, *"Verily I say unto you, that one of you shall betray me"* (verse 21). All of the disciples promised Jesus that they would be faithful to Him. We also have this same desire. Do we not *intend* to stay faithful to the Lord, even when things get rough? "I'll be faithful, no matter what," is easy to say when life is going well. But, as one man said, "A faith that cannot be tested cannot be trusted." In the lives of these disciples, the test was about to come.

In the Garden of Gethsemane, Jesus asked His disciples to wait while He went further to pray. Alone, He poured out His soul to the Father in prayer: *"O my Father, if it be possible, let this cup pass from me: nevertheless not as I will, but as thou wilt"* (verse 39). He returned from praying—not once, not twice, but three times—to find His disciples asleep. Men who were specially chosen, who had promised that they would die with Him before they would deny Him, couldn't even fulfill the simple request to *"watch and pray."* But as Jesus said (and it is true of us today as well), *"the spirit indeed is willing, but the flesh is weak"* (verse 41).

Soon the soldiers, led by Judas the traitor, came to arrest Jesus. Now was the time for the disciples to show their resolution, but *"all the disciples forsook him, and fled"* (verse 56).

The sad story continues: *"But Peter followed him afar off"* (verse 58). Peter did follow Jesus—at a safe distance. This lack of proximity could describe many Christians today; they follow Jesus to a point, but remain at a safe distance so they are sure not to get too carried away. Away from the presence of the Lord, Peter soon found himself at a place of decision.

Matthew 26:69–74

69 …a damsel came unto him, saying, Thou also wast
with Jesus of Galilee.
70 But he denied before them all, saying, I know not what
thou sayest.
71 And when he was gone out into the porch, another
maid saw him, and said unto them that were there, This
fellow was also with Jesus of Nazareth.
72 And again he denied with an oath, I do not know
the man.
73 And after a while came unto him they that stood by,
and said to Peter, Surely thou also art one of them; for thy
speech bewrayeth thee.
74 Then began he to curse and to swear, saying, I know
not the man….

Peter's denial actually began when he left the presence of Jesus. Apart from the Lord and under pressure from hostile surroundings, he denied the Lord, the second time with an oath. Then with his third denial, he cursed and swore. Shocking, is it not, that a disciple of the Lord would go this far to deny the Lord? When we distance ourselves from the Lord, there is no telling how low we will go!

Distancing ourselves from God's presence has an effect on our reputation as well. Remember the disciple we sometimes call "Doubting Thomas"? He was not with the other disciples when Jesus appeared to them after His Resurrection, and Thomas said, "*Except I shall see in his hands the print of the nails, and put my finger into the print of the nails, and thrust my hand into his side, I will not believe*" (John 20:25). Jesus later revealed Himself to Thomas (John 20:27), but Thomas certainly missed a blessing because he was not there the first time; and as a result, his reputation was set for all time. It is important as a disciple of Jesus to be present with Him.

B. To be like Him

Luke 6:40 tells us, "*The disciple is not above his master: but every one that is perfect shall be as his master.*" In this sense, the word *perfect* means "complete, one who is what he ought to be." The disciple is one who is continually becoming more like the Master.

The disciples of Jesus were like Him, and people noticed. The people around the fire charged Peter with knowing Jesus because they said "*thy speech bewrayeth thee*" (Matthew 26:73). The word *bewray* means "clear, evident, manifest." It was obvious to them that Peter was a disciple because of the way he talked. Tragically, Peter chose that moment to curse and swear in an effort to prove that he did not even know Jesus—but it was too late; his speech had already given him away. When people hear us talk, would they say, "You're one of them, a disciple of Christ; you know Jesus; we can tell by the way you talk"?

Romans 8:29

29 *For whom he did foreknow, he also did predestinate to be conformed to the image of his Son…*

Christians should strive to be like Christ—a high-quality copy which cannot be distinguished from the original. We are conformed to the image, or copied from the likeness, of the Lord Jesus Christ.

1 Corinthians 15:49

49 *And as we have borne the image of the earthy, we shall also bear the image of the heavenly.*

Colossians 3:9–10
9 *Lie not one to another, seeing that ye have put off the old man with his deeds;*
10 *And have put on the new man, which is renewed in knowledge after the image of him that created him:*

We are called to follow His example by following His steps. Let this hymn be our prayer:

O to be like Thee! blessed Redeemer,
This is my constant longing and prayer.
Gladly I'll forfeit all of earth's treasures.
Jesus, Thy perfect likeness to wear.

O to be like Thee! O to be like Thee,
Blessed Redeemer, pure as Thou art!
Come in Thy sweetness, come in Thy fullness;
Stamp Thine own image deep on my heart.

A disciple of Christ is one who is called to be with Him and called to be like Him.

II. A Disciple Is Criticized

Personal criticism is extremely hard to accept, but Jesus, the perfect Son of God, was severely criticized while He was here on this earth. Everything He did displeased the Pharisees somehow. They didn't like His healing people on the Sabbath day; they didn't like His eating with publicans and sinners; they didn't like His claiming that *"I and my Father are one"* (John 10:30); they didn't like that He did not wash before dinner, and the list could go on.

Jesus taught us to expect criticism for the sake of being His disciples and even to appreciate criticism as an honor.

Matthew 5:11–12

11 *Blessed are ye, when men shall revile you, and persecute you, and shall say all manner of evil against you falsely, for my sake.*

12 *Rejoice, and be exceeding glad: for great is your reward in heaven: for so persecuted they the prophets which were before you.*

A. Corporately

By choosing to be a disciple of Christ, you automatically align yourself with a group that is often criticized.

Illustration

The term *Christian fundamentalist* is often equated with "nut, fanatic, or extremist." A *little* religion is often respected by the world. (Every presidential candidate seems to claim that he believes in and honors God and has some sort of church affiliation.) But a person who insists that he genuinely believes the Bible, attends church regularly with Bible in hand, believes in and practices tithing, prays and expects God to answer, and witnesses to others of Christ, is generally regarded as "a few fries short of a Happy Meal."

We read in the book of Acts of the persecutions encountered by the early church. Aside from anything they did individually, early Christians were persecuted simply because they were members of the group.

Acts 8:1

1 *…And at that time there was a great persecution against the church which was at Jerusalem; and they were all scattered abroad…*

Acts 12:1

1 *Now about that time Herod the king stretched forth his hands to vex certain of the church.*

We can all relate to this concept: people tend to judge individuals by stereotyping their group. Did you ever stop to think how many different ways there are to group people? Man or woman, old or young, blond or brunette, Cubs fan or White Sox fan, and (for those who are still fighting the Civil War) Yankees or Rebels.

In Acts 24:5, an orator named Tertullus began to accuse the Apostle Paul before the Roman governor Felix, finding him "*a pestilent fellow, and a mover of sedition among all the Jews throughout the world, and a ringleader of the sect of the Nazarenes.*" These accusers called the disciples of Christ a cult. (They would probably consider fundamental Baptists a cult today as well.) Paul reports, "*Being defamed, we intreat: we are made as the filth of the world, and are the offscouring of all things unto this day*" (1 Corinthians 4:13).

Although we will be criticized, disciples of Christ ought not to be concerned about accusations. We are to be *in* the world, but not *of* the world (John 17:15). God has left us here to live for Him. As the disciples of the Lord Jesus Christ, we stand together as a group, and we need to accept that sometimes we will be criticized as a group.

B. Individually

As disciples of Christ, we will also be criticized individually. We have this promise in 2 Timothy 3:12: "*Yea, and all that will live godly in Christ Jesus shall suffer persecution.*" Living for Jesus may cause you to be criticized and persecuted—and there are times that the persecution will be personal.

Stephen, the first Christian martyr, was accused of being a blasphemer. Paul was pointed out individually as being a troublemaker. Jason, who had taken Paul in and cared for him, was persecuted for his compassion.

Naturally, we would rather not be criticized. We tend to take criticism personally and allow it to wound us, even when we know the criticism is for Christ's sake. But we need to understand that we cannot seek the friendship of the world just to avoid persecution. James 4:4 warns, "*Ye adulterers and adulteresses, know ye not that the friendship of the world is enmity with God? whosoever therefore will be a friend of the world is the enemy of God.*"

The world does not understand what it truly means to be a disciple. Because of this lack of understanding, Jesus' disciples were criticized. Be prepared for people to murmur against you if you insist on being a disciple of Christ.

Luke 5:30

30 But their scribes and Pharisees murmured against his disciples, saying, Why do ye eat and drink with publicans and sinners?

Not only will the world persecute you, but other *believers* may also criticize you for being a true disciple of Christ. This may happen for a variety of reasons. If you are more serious about living for Christ than they are, they may feel guilty, and they may react by lashing out against you. Acts 13:45 gives us an example of Jews who were jealous of Paul: "*But when the Jews saw the multitudes, they were filled with envy, and spake against those things which were spoken by Paul, contradicting and blaspheming.*" They were losing their followers to Paul, and so they went after him verbally, speaking against him, contradicting him, blaspheming, and criticizing him. Paul remained faithful in the face of criticism, just as we should.

III. A Disciple Is Commissioned

God has commissioned His disciples with specific tasks to complete.

A. To learn

The disciples had special opportunities to learn directly from the Lord Jesus. He explained things to them and taught them things that He did not share with the multitudes. Many times Jesus spoke in parables to the multitudes and Jewish leaders. And then, when alone with His own disciples, He would explain the meaning of these parables.

Mark 4:33–34
33 *And with many such parables spake he the word unto them, as they were able to hear it.*
34 *But without a parable spake he not unto them: and when they were alone, he expounded all things to his disciples.*

Matthew 13:16 shares Jesus' reasoning on giving these revelations to His disciples when He was not willing to share them with others. "*But blessed are your eyes, for they see: and your ears, for they hear.*" The disciples wanted His teaching. They craved it. Many times in Scripture we see them asking Jesus for the meaning of a concept. On one special occasion, they asked Him to teach them to pray.

As time went on, Jesus spent increasingly more time teaching His disciples about the future. In Mark 9:31–32, Jesus explained the Gospel to the disciples: "*For he taught his disciples, and said unto them, The Son of man is delivered into the hands of men, and they shall kill him; and after that he is killed, he shall rise the third day. But they understood not that saying, and were afraid to ask him.*"

On another occasion, in Matthew 24, the disciples specifically asked for the meaning behind the prophecies, and Jesus explained to them what will happen in the last days. So the disciples of Christ truly were His pupils, and their major responsibility during those three short years of ministry was to listen and learn from Jesus' teaching.

After His Resurrection, Christ continued to teach, not just to the twelve, but also to His other followers, such as the two men on the road to Emmaus (Luke 24:13–31). Before Christ ascended back to His Father, He made sure to tell the disciples that they would always have a Heavenly Teacher: "*But the Comforter, which is the Holy Ghost, whom the Father will send in my name, he shall teach you all things, and bring all things to your remembrance, whatsoever I have said unto you*" (John 14:26). The learning process of the disciples never ended, and so it should be with us today. All of us need to be "lifelong learners."

As educated and as spiritually mature as Paul was, he still felt the need to continue learning—even in prison when he knew he would not get out alive! In 2 Timothy 4:13, he made a special request for "*the books, but especially the parchments.*" If the Apostle Paul, after writing fourteen books of the New Testament, still felt that he should study and learn, how much the more should we!

TEACHING TIP

Take a moment to remind your students of all the opportunities they have to learn. In an enthusiastic, Bible-believing church, there are many opportunities to learn the Word of God. Remind your students of the work put into each sermon, Bible study, and lesson. Having godly pastors and teachers who are truly "apt [skillful] to teach" (2 Timothy 2:24) is a tremendous blessing, and church members need to be just as eager and skillful to learn.

B. To tell

As disciples of Christ, we have a commission to learn, but we also have a commission to tell.

Luke 9:1–6

1 *Then he called his twelve disciples together, and gave them power and authority over all devils, and to cure diseases.*

2 *And he sent them to preach the kingdom of God, and to heal the sick.*

3 *And he said unto them, Take nothing for your journey, neither staves, nor scrip, neither bread, neither money; neither have two coats apiece.*

4 *And whatsoever house ye enter into, there abide, and thence depart.*

5 *And whosoever will not receive you, when ye go out of that city, shake off the very dust from your feet for a testimony against them.*

6 *And they departed, and went through the towns, preaching the gospel, and healing every where.*

The disciples had learned many things from Jesus Christ, and now He was sending them out to tell others what they had learned. Although we never stop learning and growing, we have a responsibility to share what we have already learned.

At the empty tomb that first Sunday morning, the angel told the women who came to tend to Jesus' body, "*And go quickly, and tell his disciples that he is risen from the dead; and, behold, he goeth before you into Galilee; there shall ye see him: lo, I have told you*" (Matthew 28:7). Jesus wanted His disciples to know that He was risen.

Later in that same chapter we have the Great Commission: "*Go ye therefore, and teach all nations, baptizing them in the name of the Father, and of the Son, and of the Holy Ghost: Teaching them to observe all things whatsoever I have commanded you: and, lo, I am with you alway, even unto the end of the world. Amen*" (Matthew 28:19–20). Christ wanted His disciples to pass on the good news, just as He wants us to pass it on today.

The early church took this commission very seriously. The High Priest accused the apostles of "*filling Jerusalem*" with the doctrine of Christ. The faithful witness of the apostles was widely effective in Jerusalem, and the book of Acts offers the continuing story of how the Gospel began to spread across the world. The last recorded words of Jesus before His ascension were these: "*But ye shall receive power, after that the Holy Ghost is come upon you: and ye shall be witnesses unto me both in Jerusalem, and in all Judaea, and in Samaria, and unto the uttermost part of the earth*" (Acts 1:8). This was the commission given to the disciples: to tell.

This commission to tell others about Christ was not only given to that special group. Many examples are included in the Scriptures of ordinary people who had seen the Lord do extraordinary things for them and wanted to tell others:

The woman at the well—John 4:28–29
The maniac of Gadara—Mark 5:19
The men on the road to Emmaus—Luke 24:32–35

So, as disciples of the Lord, we also have a commission and, more than that, a privilege to tell others about Christ. Jesus said in Matthew 10:32–33, "*Whosoever therefore shall confess me before men, him will I confess also before my Father which is in heaven. But whosoever shall deny me before men, him will I also deny before my Father which is in heaven.*"

The word *confess* here means "to declare openly, speak out freely, to profess one's self the worshipper of [Christ]." The word *deny* means "to disclaim" (as when Peter denied Christ). The concept is clear, is it not? If we will speak up for Jesus before men, He will speak up for us before His Father. If we refuse to speak up for Him, or worse, if we give in to fear and actually deny Him out loud, He will deny us before His Father.

Most commentators see Christ as an advocate asking for the answer to our prayers. When we speak up for Him, He speaks up for us (2 Timothy 2:12, 13).

Illustration

We must be watchful of our attitudes. Sometimes disciples can hinder people from coming to Christ. Jesus' disciples actually tried to keep people away from Him! In Mark 10:13, we read, "*And they brought young children to him, that he should touch them: and his disciples rebuked those that brought them."*

We must never view people as inconveniences even when we are required to suffer inconveniences for the sake of allowing people to hear the Word of God. Are you willing, for example, to give up your seat in church to a visitor?

Conclusion

Disciples of Christ are called, criticized, and commissioned. Are we the disciples of Christ that we ought to be? As His disciples, two distinct characteristics must be seen in our lives—rejoicing (Luke 19:37) and fruit-bearing (John 15:8). Truly, we have seen God's mighty works; let's be sure to rejoice over them and to praise God for the opportunity and privilege of being His disciples.

Study Questions

1. What does the word *disciple* mean?
   The word disciple means "learner" or "pupil."

2. When did Peter's denial of Jesus Christ actually begin?
   Peter's denial of Christ actually began when he left the presence of Jesus.

3. What characteristic of Peter did those at the fire recognize that identified him with Jesus?
   Peter's speech was evidence to them that he had been with Jesus.

4. In what two ways may Christians be criticized for Christ?
   Christians may be criticized: corporately (as a group) and individually (personally).

5. Christ wants us to be continually aware of His presence and to open every area of our lives to Him. Has He convicted you of areas you have closed off to Him? If so, what areas?
   Answers will vary.

6. How can you respond to both corporate and individual criticism in a godly way?
   Answers will vary but could include the following: refuse to make it personal, recite Scripture, pray for your accusers.

7. A disciple has been commissioned by Christ to learn. What is something you are learning/have learned over the past month?
   Answers will vary.

8. With whom did you share the Gospel this past week? Who will you share it with this week?
   Answers will vary.

Memory Verse

John 13:35

35 *By this shall all men know that ye are my disciples, if ye have love one to another.*

LESSON NINE

The Bride of Christ

Text

Ephesians 5:25–32

25 Husbands, love your wives, even as Christ also loved the
church, and gave himself for it;
26 That he might sanctify and cleanse it with the washing of
water by the word,
27 That he might present it to himself a glorious church, not
having spot, or wrinkle, or any such thing; but that it should
be holy and without blemish.
28 So ought men to love their wives as their own bodies. He
that loveth his wife loveth himself.
29 For no man ever yet hated his own flesh; but nourisheth
and cherisheth it, even as the Lord the church:
30 For we are members of his body, of his flesh, and of
his bones.
31 For this cause shall a man leave his father and mother, and
shall be joined unto his wife, and they two shall be one flesh.
32 This is a great mystery: but I speak concerning Christ and
the church.

Overview

Christ compares the church to a bride, a symbol of a pure love. He desires that we, as Christians, would come to Him in the same way that a bride comes to her groom, "*holy and without blemish*" (verse 27). Our proper response to our Groom (Jesus Christ) is to love Him in return for His action of love on Calvary.

Lesson Theme

Christ, our groom, continually showers us with His all-encompassing love. As His bride, we must prepare ourselves for His coming by *"not having spot, or wrinkle."* We must keep ourselves holy while awaiting His return.

Lesson Objectives

At the conclusion of the lesson, each student should:

1. Surrender to the work of the Groom in their lives in preparation for His return.
2. Understand the need for inner purity that honors the Groom with external manifestations of purity.
3. Look expectantly toward Christ's return with patience and trust.

Teaching Outline

Introduction

I. Preparation
 A. Of heart
 B. Of self

II. Purity
 A. Outward
 B. Inward

III. Patience
 A. In waiting for Christ
 B. Toward all men
 C. In tribulation

Conclusion

LESSON NINE

The Bride of Christ

Text

EPHESIANS 5:25–32

25 *Husbands, love your wives, even as Christ also loved the church, and gave himself for it;*

26 *That he might sanctify and cleanse it with the washing of water by the word,*

27 *That he might present it to himself a glorious church, not having spot, or wrinkle, or any such thing; but that it should be holy and without blemish.*

28 *So ought men to love their wives as their own bodies. He that loveth his wife loveth himself.*

29 *For no man ever yet hated his own flesh; but nourisheth and cherisheth it, even as the Lord the church:*

30 *For we are members of his body, of his flesh, and of his bones.*

31 *For this cause shall a man leave his father and mother, and shall be joined unto his wife, and they two shall be one flesh.*

32 *This is a great mystery: but I speak concerning Christ and the church.*

Introduction

A bride is a beautiful symbol of pure love. A bride revels in giving her love to her groom—and having that love returned. Our key verses compare the church to a bride. God, the Person of love (1 John 4:8) and our Groom, has expressed His love for us in many ways, the most important being a sacrificial provision for our salvation. Our proper response to God's love is to love Him in return. First John 4:19 reveals, "*We love him, because he first loved us.*" True love is much more than just an emotion (the way we feel); it is a verb (an action). God's love for His people is indeed overwhelming when we see His action of love.

Romans 5:8
8 *But God commendeth* [showed, proved, exhibited] *his love toward us, in that, while we were yet sinners, Christ died for us.*

Certain characteristics come to the forefront as we look at a bride.

I. Preparation

A wedding is a glorious time, and it usually involves an incredible amount of preparation for the "big day." There are so many details: decorations, travel arrangements, invitations, food, dress, etc.

Illustration

Many years ago, I was the best man at my friend's wedding and found myself quite unprepared. My friend had not given me enough notice of the schedule, so I was unable to attend his wedding rehearsal. This meant that I went into the ceremony not too sure of what I was supposed to do or where I was supposed to be. Even worse, while dressing for the wedding, with less than an hour until the ceremony, I discovered that my rented formalwear was missing a tie! I will not tell you how fast I drove to the formalwear store and back to the church (in case the statute of limitations has not run out), but I did make it back to the church in time and managed to get through the ceremony somehow. (In spite of the lack of preparation, God has blessed: this couple recently celebrated their twenty-fifth anniversary, and they have put two girls through our college. My friend and I have remained friends all these years!)

With the myriad of details involved in a wedding, preparation is very important. A bride wants this special day to be perfect. The Bible speaks of the preparation of the bride of Christ. If we love the Lord Jesus, we will want to be properly prepared when we see Him. This preparation does not happen by accident, nor can it be a hurried matter. Our preparation as Christ's bride begins at salvation with the forgiveness of our sins and is carried forward with our surrender to His will.

Romans 12:1–2

1 *I beseech you therefore, brethren, by the mercies of God, that ye present your bodies a living sacrifice, holy, acceptable unto God, which is your reasonable service.*

2 *And be not conformed to this world: but be ye transformed by the renewing of your mind, that ye may prove what is that good, and acceptable, and perfect, will of God.*

We prepare for our Heavenly Bridegroom by daily surrendering to the working of God in our lives. It is our "reasonable service" to surrender ourselves as a "living sacrifice," with no will of our own—not conforming to the standards of the world, but rather being transformed by allowing the Word of God to permeate our minds and make us more and more what Christ would have us to be.

A. *Of heart*

The bride prepares her heart for the bridegroom. She looks forward to the wedding for many months ahead of time. She doodles as she talks on the phone, "Mrs. _____." She dreams about how wonderful the marriage will be. She prepares her heart.

We must prepare our hearts for the Lord with this same passion. First Samuel 7:3 tells how Samuel asks God's people to, *"prepare your hearts unto the Lord, and serve him only."* Commentator Matthew Henry explains that phrase this way: "make a solemn business of returning to God, and do it with a serious consideration and a stedfast resolution." We must not come to God lightly or flippantly; we must take the matter of coming into His presence very seriously and very reverently.

When Moses, an escaped criminal from Egypt, was on the backside of the desert tending the flocks of his father-in-law, he saw a burning bush. He went to investigate and found himself in the very presence of God. *"And when the Lord saw that he turned aside to see, God called unto him out of the midst of the bush, and said, …I am the God of thy father, the God of Abraham, the God of Isaac, and the God of Jacob. And Moses hid his face; for he was afraid to look upon God"* (Exodus 3:4–6). Moses realized the awful solemnity of the presence of God.

We need to realize who God is, and we need to realize who we are. Moses asked God, "*Who am I, that I should go unto Pharaoh, and that I should bring forth the children of Israel out of Egypt?*" (Exodus 3:11). David asked, "*Who am I, O Lord God? and what is my house, that thou hast brought me hitherto?*" (2 Samuel 7:18). Solomon asked, "*But who am I, and what is my people, that we should be able to offer so willingly after this sort?*" (1 Chronicles 29:14).

So, who am I?

- **A unique creation of God** (Psalm 139:14–16)
- **A sinner by nature and by choice** (Romans 5:12)
- **Valuable to God** (John 3:16–17; 1 Corinthians 6:20)
- **Someone God wants to use** (1 Corinthians 15:10; Philippians 2:13)

The preparation of the heart of a believer begins with the realization of who God really is and who we really are.

In the parable of ten virgins, five prepared themselves for the coming of the groom, and five did not.

Matthew 25:1–13

1 *Then shall the kingdom of heaven be likened unto ten virgins, which took their lamps, and went forth to meet the bridegroom.*

2 *And five of them were wise, and five were foolish.*

3 *They that were foolish took their lamps, and took no oil with them:*

4 *But the wise took oil in their vessels with their lamps.*

5 *While the bridegroom tarried, they all slumbered and slept.*

6 *And at midnight there was a cry made, Behold, the
bridegroom cometh; go ye out to meet him.*
7 *Then all those virgins arose, and trimmed their lamps.*
8 *And the foolish said unto the wise, Give us of your oil;
for our lamps are gone out.*
9 *But the wise answered, saying, Not so; lest there be not
enough for us and you: but go ye rather to them that sell,
and buy for yourselves.*
10 *And while they went to buy, the bridegroom came; and
they that were ready went in with him to the marriage:
and the door was shut.*
11 *Afterward came also the other virgins, saying, Lord,
Lord, open to us.*
12 *But he answered and said, Verily I say unto you, I know
you not.*
13 *Watch therefore, for ye know neither the day nor the
hour wherein the Son of man cometh.*

For the five virgins who did not prepare, a day came when it was just too late. They had put off the preparation too long. We, too, must prepare our hearts to meet the Lord. Will He find us prepared when He returns?

An old hymn, written by Fanny Crosby, reminds us to prepare our hearts for the Lord:

When Jesus comes to reward His servants,
Whether it be noon or night,
Faithful to Him will He find us watching,
With our lamps all trimmed and bright?

Oh, can we say we are ready, brother?
Ready for the soul's bright home?
Say, will He find you and me still watching,
Waiting, waiting when the Lord shall come?

Deuteronomy 4:29

29 But if from thence thou shalt seek the Lord thy God, thou shalt find him, if thou seek him with all thy heart and with all thy soul.

The bride prepares her heart for her bridegroom. She spends much time thinking about him and longs to be with him. We likewise need to prepare our hearts for the Lord.

B. Of self

The bride takes much care preparing herself for her wedding. Months ahead of the special day she selects the "perfect" wedding dress. She picks out just the right veil, the right bouquet, and the right jewelry. Her hair has to be just right. She takes extra care on her makeup. Every once in awhile, a story about a "Bridezilla" will appear on the news or surface on the internet—a bride who literally goes berserk when something goes wrong with the last-minute preparations for the wedding. These stories are very funny—unless you are personally involved!

As the bride of Christ, we need to prepare ourselves. Our lives ought to be pleasing to Him. We need to make sure we are living according to His will. We don't want to be ashamed when we see Him.

1 John 2:28

28 And now, little children, abide in him; that, when he shall appear, we may have confidence, and not be ashamed before him at his coming.

Luke 12:40

40 Be ye therefore ready also: for the Son of man cometh at an hour when ye think not.

Be prepared! If we are living in such a way that we would not be ashamed were He to return any moment, our joy when seeing Him will be great. "*Let us be glad and rejoice, and give honour to him: for the marriage of the Lamb is come, and his wife hath made herself ready*" (Revelation 19:7).

II. Purity

The symbolism of a white wedding dress is familiar but important: the purity of the bride, set apart for her husband. The Lord desires and expects purity from *His* bride as well.

TEACHING TIP

If possible, bring a wedding dress with you to class to visually capture your students' attention. A bit later in the lesson when you begin teaching about the importance of both inner and outer purity, you can remind your students that the most beautiful wedding dress is worn by the bride who wears it to symbolize a true inner purity.

It is very important to the Lord that His people be clean and pure. Throughout the Old Testament, this truth is repeated.

Ezra 6:20 records the reinstitution of the Passover with God's people who had come out of captivity: "*For the priests and the Levites were **purified** together, all of them were pure, and killed the passover for all the children of the captivity, and for their brethren the priests, and for themselves.*"

Nehemiah 12:30 tells of the dedication of the wall of Jerusalem: "*And the priests and the Levites purified themselves, and **purified** the people, and the gates, and the wall.*"

In Psalm 51, David repented of his sin and pled with God for cleansing and purity:

"Wash me throughly from mine iniquity, and cleanse me from my sin" (verse 2).

"Purge me with hyssop, and I shall be clean: wash me, and I shall be whiter than snow" (verse 7).

"Create in me a clean heart, O God; and renew a right spirit within me" (verse 10).

A. *Outward*

Wedding guests usually stand as the bride enters the room, honoring her as she makes her way to the altar and her waiting groom. All admire her beauty and grace and spotless white wedding dress. What would people think if she romped down the aisle wearing old dirty clothes with her hair messed up and popping bubble gum? Her outward appearance would be inappropriate for the occasion. Our outward appearance—our dress, speech, and actions—needs to be pure and honoring to the Lord.

Illustration

Mark 1:40–41 gives an account of a leper who came to Jesus in desperation and told Him, *"If thou wilt, thou canst make me clean. And Jesus, moved with compassion, put forth his hand, and touched him, and saith unto him, I will; be thou clean."* The man was pleading to be made clean and pure, and without hesitation, Jesus granted that request. Do we desire purity as much as that leper did?

Leprosy is a bacterial infection, which can destroy both nerves and tissues and result in various deformities. This disease still exists in the modern world. According to the 2003 edition of *Encyclopaedia Britannica*, "Reported cases of leprosy throughout the world number at least 2,000,000, and the actual number of infected persons may be as high as 11,000,000." The following passage gives us an idea of the lifestyle a leper was forced to lead.

Leviticus 13:45–46

45 *And the leper in whom the plague is, his clothes shall be rent, and his head bare, and he shall put a covering upon his upper lip, and shall cry, Unclean, unclean.*

46 *All the days wherein the plague shall be in him he shall be defiled; he is unclean: he shall dwell alone; without the camp shall his habitation be.*

In addition to the physical suffering itself, a leper had to live in this manner! No wonder the leper came to Jesus and beseeched Him to make him clean.

Leprosy is a picture of sin. Sin always manifests itself outwardly, eventually. As Christians, we need to honor God with our outward appearance. Some people use the verse "*...man looketh on the outward appearance, but the Lord looketh on the heart*" (1 Samuel 16:7) to teach that the outward appearance is not important. That is twisting the Scripture—both inward and outward are important. It *does* matter how we dress, how we talk, and how we act.

Matthew Henry says this: "He who is not shy of the appearances of sin, who shuns not the occasions of sin, and who avoids not the temptations and approaches to sin, will not long abstain from the actual commission of sin."

So there is an outward purity that is very important, for the bride and for the Christian.

B. Inward

Outward purity can be faked for a time; it is possible to act and look right for a while, without being right inside.

Illustration

Every West Coast Baptist College student *looks* right on the outside because the rules of the school require it and because those rules are enforced. The state of the heart, however, may be different. It is not always possible to determine the inner character by the outward appearance, but eventually the heart that is not right with God will be revealed. The truth will come out, good or bad.

Our outward appearance is supposed to be clean and pure, but we must not just be satisfied with looking right. *Looking* right is no substitute for *being* right.

May I remind you that Judas Iscariot was one of the disciples of Christ? He looked right; he went out and preached and ministered with the others; he saw the miracles of Jesus and heard His preaching and teaching; he was even made the treasurer of the group (John 13:29). But the sinfulness of his heart and his surrender to Satan eventually came out as he betrayed the Lord and then died a miserable, messy suicide (Matthew 27:3–5; Acts 1:15–18).

James 4:8

8 ...Cleanse your hands, ye sinners; and purify your hearts, ye double minded.

Not only cleanse your hands—look right on the outside, but purify your hearts—be right on the inside. That which is in the heart, will come out in the life.

PROVERBS 4:23

23 *Keep thy heart with all diligence; for out of it are the issues of life.*

In Matthew 15:18–20 Jesus said, "*...those things which proceed out of the mouth come forth from the heart; and they defile the man. For out of the heart proceed evil thoughts, murders, adulteries, fornications, thefts, false witness, blasphemies: These are the things which defile a man....*"

Sincere outward purity is a result of genuine inward purity.

III. Patience

Patience is an essential virtue for a bride as the engagement period normally lasts several months.

Illustration

A friend of mine has refused to allow his daughters to marry until both the daughter and the fiancé have graduated from college. Both young people understand that he has their best interests at heart and have respected his wishes, but the waiting surely is an exercise in patience.

Part of the fruit of the Spirit is "longsuffering" (Galatians 5:22–23). This word means "patience, endurance, constancy, steadfastness, perseverance." I've often heard great leaders say that the three greatest abilities are "availability, dependability, and stickability." We need to have that quality of "stickability" for the Lord.

Romans 2:6–7

6 [God] *will render to every man according to his deeds:*
7 *To them who by* ***patient continuance in well doing*** *seek for glory and honour and immortality, eternal life:*

Galatians 6:8–9

8 *...he that soweth to the Spirit shall of the Spirit reap life everlasting.*
9 *And* ***let us not be weary in well doing****: for in due season we shall reap, if we faint not.*

2 Thessalonians 3:13

13 *But ye, brethren,* ***be not weary in well doing****.*

1 Corinthians 15:58

58 *Therefore, my beloved brethren,* ***be ye stedfast, unmoveable, always abounding in the work of the Lord****, forasmuch as ye know that your labour is not in vain in the Lord.*

Patience! The bride is to be patient as she prepares and looks forward to the wedding; we as believers need to be patient as we live for the Lord and wait for His coming.

A. *In waiting for Christ*

2 Thessalonians 3:5

5 *And the Lord direct your hearts into the love of God, and into the patient waiting for Christ.*

We wait in patient expectation of Christ's Second Coming.

James 5:7–8

7 *Be patient therefore, brethren, unto the coming of the Lord. Behold, the husbandman waiteth for the precious fruit of the earth, and hath long patience for it, until he receive the early and latter rain.*

8 *Be ye also patient; stablish your hearts: for the coming of the Lord draweth nigh.*

We also must patiently wait for the Lord to do His work in situations where we are tempted to think He is taking too long. Many times, we have "a will for God's life," and we believe we know exactly what He should do. But His ways are not our ways and His thoughts are higher than our thoughts (Isaiah 55:9).

The Lord does not have to work on our timetable or our schedule. He does not need to do things the way we think they ought to be done. When we wait on Him, we learn that His way is far better than ours.

Second Kings 5:1–14 relates the story of Naaman, captain of the host of the king of Syria, who was stricken with leprosy. When Elisha sent him a message to "*wash in Jordan seven times...and thou shalt be clean,*" Naaman grew angry. He thought that Elisha would "*surely come out to me, and stand, and call on the name of the LORD his God, and strike his hand over the place, and recover the leper.*" He almost missed being healed because it was not done the way he thought it should have been done. God's way maybe wasn't as dramatic as the way Naaman would have chosen, but it worked! As a result, God, rather than Naaman, got the glory.

In John 11, we read the story of Lazarus, who was sick. His sisters sent word to Jesus asking Him to come. Jesus could have come as the sisters had requested, but He stayed right where He was for two more days. When He finally arrived, Lazarus was dead. As far as the sisters were concerned, Jesus was too late. They both told Him, "*Lord, if thou hadst been here, my brother had not died.*" You know the rest of the story—Jesus raised Lazarus from the dead. Jesus did not do what Mary and Martha thought He should have done, but in the end, He did exactly what was right.

Waiting for the Lord to work in our lives is frequently more difficult than taking matters into our own hands. We are often tempted to say, "Let's *do* something, even if it's wrong!" Inaction in times of stress and crisis goes against our nature, but we have to realize that our nature often goes against God.

Jesus, in Gethsemane, told His disciples, "*My soul is exceeding sorrowful, even unto death: tarry ye here, and watch with me*" (Matthew 26:38). They couldn't wait and watch; they gave up and fell asleep. As Christ told his disciples to tarry and wait, sometimes we need to be patient and wait.

The psalmist says in Psalm 27:14, "*Wait on the Lord: be of good courage, and he shall strengthen thine heart: wait, I say, on the Lord.*"

B. Toward all men

1 Thessalonians 5:14

14 Now we exhort you, brethren, warn them that are unruly, comfort the feebleminded, support the weak, be patient toward all men.

Patience with people is not something that comes easily. We hate waiting—whether for the checkout line, congested traffic, or a table at a restaurant. We hate waiting for people. Yes, schedules are a good thing, but we ought not to feel that our time is more important than anyone else's time.

James 4:14 reminds us, "*For what is your life? It is even a vapour, that appeareth for a little time, and then vanisheth away.*" Ministering to other people is one reason that God has placed us in this world instead of taking us Home, and yet many times we are so busy that we run right by other people. We rejoice that God is so patient with us, don't we? We also appreciate it when other people are patient with us? However, we often struggle when we need to be patient with others.

We have a hard time being patient when people **mistreat** us. We need to remember the words of Christ:

Matthew 5:44

44 *...Love your enemies, bless them that curse you, do good to them that hate you, and pray for them which despitefully use you, and persecute you.*

We also have a hard time being patient when we are **misunderstood**.

1 Peter 2:19–20

19 *For this is thankworthy, if a man for conscience toward God endure grief, suffering wrongfully.*
20 *For what glory is it, if, when ye be buffeted for your faults, ye shall take it patiently? but if, when ye do well, and suffer for it, ye take it patiently, this is acceptable with God.*

Finally, we have a hard time being patient when it comes to **being willing to stop and listen** to others.

James 1:19

19 *Wherefore, my beloved brethren, let every man be swift to hear, slow to speak, slow to wrath.*

C. In tribulation

Romans 12:12

12 *Rejoicing in hope; patient in tribulation; continuing instant in prayer.*

To be patient in tribulation, according to Strong, means "under misfortunes and trials to hold fast to one's faith in Christ."

REVELATION 14:12

12 *Here is the patience of the saints: here are they that keep the commandments of God, and the faith of Jesus.*

- **Job**
  God specially pointed out Job, as the godliest man in the whole world, to Satan: *"Hast thou considered my servant Job, that there is none like him in the earth, a perfect and an upright man, one that feareth God, and escheweth evil?"* (Job 1:8). God permitted Satan to take away just about everything Job had except for his life, and Job said, "*...the LORD gave, and the LORD hath taken away; blessed be the name of the LORD*" (Job 1:21). Job's faithfulness was tested, but he kept the faith during his trials and tribulations.

- **Joseph**
  Sold as a slave into Egypt by his own brothers, Joseph, after being falsely accused, was thrown into jail. In every situation, Joseph remained faithful. God used him to preserve his family and the lineage of Christ. Joseph said to his brothers, *"But as for you, ye thought evil against me; but God meant it unto good, to bring to pass, as it is this day, to save much people alive"* (Genesis 50:20).

- **Paul**
  Familiar with frequent, intense tribulation, Paul faithfully continued in ministry. He summarized the obstacles he faced and the burdens he carried in 2 Corinthians 11:23–28: "*...in labours more abundant,*

in stripes above measure, in prisons more frequent, in deaths oft. Of the Jews five times received I forty stripes save one. Thrice was I beaten with rods, once was I stoned, thrice I suffered shipwreck, a night and a day I have been in the deep; In journeyings often, in perils of waters, in perils of robbers, in perils by mine own countrymen, in perils by the heathen, in perils in the city, in perils in the wilderness, in perils in the sea, in perils among false brethren; In weariness and painfulness, in watchings often, in hunger and thirst, in fastings often, in cold and nakedness. Beside those things that are without, that which cometh upon me daily, the care of all the churches." Patience is what enabled Paul to persevere and "*press toward the mark for the prize of the high calling of God in Christ Jesus*" (Philippians 3:14).

Patience in tribulation reveals a dependence on God. Remember that He is in control all the way through.

Conclusion

What a privilege to be the bride of Christ! With such a privilege, we should prepare diligently for His return. Ask Him to search your heart and life for any impurity that is displeasing and dishonoring to Him. Wait patiently for Him to unfold His plan in your life through even unpleasant situations. Most of all, look expectantly for His return.

Study Questions

1. In what three ways are we to emulate a bride?
We are to emulate a bride by preparing ourselves, purifying ourselves, and being patient for the coming of our Groom.

2. What parable in Matthew 5 teaches that we must prepare our hearts for Christ?
The parable of the ten virgins illustrates the preparation of our hearts for Christ.

3. What disease, prevalent in Bible times, portrays the damage of sin in a person's life?
Leprosy is a picture of sin.

4. Which fruit of the Spirit in Galatians 5:22–23 is exemplified by patience?
Longsuffering exemplifies patience.

5. If Christ were to return right now, would you have reason to be ashamed? What can you do this week to prepare for His coming?
Answers will vary. Ideas to prepare for Christ's coming may include the following: deal with a specific sin in my life, right a damaged relationship with a brother or sister in Christ or an authority, lead someone to the Lord, find a place to serve in my church.

6. Has the Lord convicted you of an area of inner impurity that you may be masking with outer purity? What steps of action should you take to have both inner and outer purity?
   Answers will vary.

7. Describe a difficult situation in your life (possibly occurring currently) in which you need to trust God's timing. What are some practical ways you can remind yourself that His way is best when you are tempted toward impatience?
   Answers will vary. Ideas for ways to remind oneself that God's way is best may include the following: memorizing and/or displaying Scripture verses that reinforce this truth (possibly even verses from this lesson), reminding myself that my feelings are not greater than God's truth, making a conscious choice to trust God.

8. Do you give to those around you the same patience you appreciate in others toward you?
   Answers will vary.

Memory Verse

1 John 2:28

28 And now, little children, abide in him; that, when he shall appear, we may have confidence, and not be ashamed before him at his coming.

LESSON TEN

The Servant of Christ

Text

1 SAMUEL 12:24
24 Only fear the LORD, and serve him in truth with all your heart: for consider how great things he hath done for you.

Overview

The attitude of a servant has two spheres: what he is supposed to be (inward qualities) and what he is supposed to do (outward actions). When he strives to be who he is supposed to be, it will be much easier to do what he is supposed to do.

Lesson Theme

The concept of being a servant is an indispensable part of the Christian walk. Faithful, whole-hearted service is the joyous privilege of God's children.

Lesson Objectives

At the conclusion of the lesson, each student should:

1. Understand the relation between inward qualities of a servant that produce outward actions of service.
2. Determine to serve the Lord whole-heartedly and enthusiastically.

3. Wholly offer themselves as obedient, diligent, faithful servants to the Lord.

Teaching Outline

Introduction

I. Inward Qualities of a Servant of the Lord
   A. Whole-hearted service
   B. Loving
   C. Humble
   D. Joyful

II. Outward Qualities of a Servant of the Lord
   A. Obedient in his actions
   B. Diligent in his duties
   C. Faithful in his responsibilities

Conclusion

LESSON TEN

The Servant of Christ

Text

1 SAMUEL 12:24

24 Only fear the LORD, *and serve him in truth with all your heart: for consider how great things he hath done for you.*

Introduction

The concept of being a servant is an indispensable part of the Christian walk. Even if we lack other desirable personal qualities, we must have the attitude of a servant to please Christ. The attitude of a servant has two spheres: what he is supposed to *be* (inward qualities) and what he is supposed to *do* (outward actions).

The word *servant* is one of the most accurate descriptions of our Lord Jesus. One biblical synonym for the word *servant* is "minister."

Mark 10:45

45 For even the Son of man came not to be ministered unto, but to minister, and to give his life a ransom for many.

I. Inward Qualities of a Servant of the Lord

A. *Whole-hearted service*

Our key verse emphasizes two important aspects regarding our service for the Lord:

- Serve Him **in truth**—in sincerity, not just in show.
- Serve Him **with all your heart**—wholeheartedly, not half-heartedly.

Joshua 22:5

5 But take diligent heed to do the commandment and the law, which Moses the servant of the Lord charged you, to love the Lord your God, and to walk in all his ways, and to keep his commandments, and to cleave unto him, and ***to serve him with all your heart and with all your soul.***

The generations that followed Joshua's generation resisted serving the Lord consistently. They *"knew not the Lord, nor yet the works which he had done for Israel"* (Judges 2:10), but instead entered a cycle of sin and idolatry: first God's wrath and judgment, then captivity and suffering, eventually followed by sorrow and repentance, and finally God's deliverance and restoration. After a time, God's people would return to serving other gods, and the cycle would begin all over again. Their example reminds us that God's people need to serve God with their whole hearts, or eventually they will cease serving Him altogether.

In 1 Chronicles 28:9, David charges his son Solomon: "*...know thou the God of thy father, and* ***serve him with a perfect heart*** *and with a willing mind....*" The "*perfect heart*" here refers to an undivided, unwavering, committed heart.

A whole-hearted servant of God is to be loyal. Paul instructed Timothy, "*Let as many servants as are under the yoke count their own masters worthy of all honour, that the name of God and his doctrine be not blasphemed*" (1 Timothy 6:1). A servant has one master, and to that one master he is responsible to give all honor and allegiance.

Matthew 6:24

24 No man can serve two masters: for either he will hate the one, and love the other; or else he will hold to the one, and despise the other. Ye cannot serve God and mammon.

It is not possible to have a divided heart when it comes to serving God. The whole-hearted servant of God is one who is loyal to God and does not try to serve the world as well.

Illustrations

1. In 1920, several players from the Chicago White Sox were accused of taking bribes from gamblers and deliberately losing the previous year's World Series. The "Black Sox" scandal resulted in eight players being banned from the game for life.

2. During World War II, a woman known as "Tokyo Rose," through propaganda radio broadcasts, struck at the morale of the American servicemen. An American

citizen of Japanese descent (born in Los Angeles and holding an earned degree from UCLA), she was convicted of treason after the war ended. [Source: *World Book 2001*, CD-ROM edition]

3. "Axis Sally," a native of Ohio, was responsible for supporting the German Nazis in the same way that Tokyo Rose supported the Japanese. [Source: *World Book 2001*, CD-ROM edition]

4. "Hanoi Jane" (Jane Fonda), well-known actress and daughter of Henry Fonda, openly supported the Communist regime of North Vietnam during the Vietnam War.

Fitting examples of disloyalty are also found in the Bible.

- Korah rebelled against Moses and Aaron (Numbers 16). God opened up the earth, and Korah and his gang were swallowed alive into the pit.
- Absalom rebelled against his father David and tried to take the throne for himself (2 Samuel 15–18).
- Judas Iscariot betrayed Jesus Christ for thirty pieces of silver (Matthew 27:3–5).

There are also those in the Bible who were loyal to the Lord when it wasn't easy or safe.

- Daniel refused to defile himself with the king's meat and drink and was willing to trust God (Daniel 1). Later, for the sake of loyalty to God, he was willing to enter the den of lions (Daniel 6).
- Shadrach, Meshach, and Abednego refused to worship the golden image of Nebuchadnezzar

and were thrown into the burning fiery furnace (Daniel 3).

- The Hall of Faith (Hebrews 11) records the stories of many saints who were rewarded for their loyalty by miraculous acts of deliverance. That same passage also tells of others who suffered great trials and death.

The Lord Jesus' temptation in the wilderness included this answer to Satan: *"Get thee behind me, Satan: for it is written, Thou shalt worship the Lord thy God, and him only shalt thou serve"* (Luke 4:8).

A whole-hearted servant of the Lord is loyal to Him. Are we loyal to our Lord Jesus Christ, even when demonstrating that loyalty is costly?

B. Loving

Servants have a variety of motives for continuing in their position. Some are paid for it, some enjoy the appreciation, some hope the service will be returned to them somewhere down the road. But those who serve out of love know the highest motivation for rendered service. They are among those who are most Christlike. The Lord Jesus Christ's motive of love moved Him to make the ultimate sacrifice. He chose the Cross because He loved us. Titus 2:14 says that Christ *"gave himself for us."* This is the highest example of service.

We are to follow His example. Galatians 5:13 encourages us to *"by love serve one another."* We serve Christ by serving others, and we serve to the highest effectiveness when we serve out of love as He did.

C. *Humble*

In a day when self-esteem is deemed essential for success, humility is a quality in short supply.

HEBREWS 12:28

28 ...let us have grace, whereby we may serve God acceptably with reverence and godly fear.

We need to serve God with reverence and with our eyes on Him rather than on ourselves. We think too much of ourselves and too little of God.

MARK 9:33–35 relates a rather amusing story:

33 *And he came to Capernaum: and being in the house he asked them, What was it that ye disputed among yourselves by the way?*
34 *But they held their peace: for by the way they had disputed among themselves, who should be the greatest.*

Christ already knew the subject of the disciples' discussion, but He wanted their admission. They were ashamed because their pride was showing, but Jesus kindly set them straight on true greatness.

35 *And he sat down, and called the twelve, and saith unto them, If any man desire to be first, the same shall be last of all, and servant of all.*

In the very next chapter, Jesus had to repeat this same principle to James and John.

MARK 10:43–45

43 *...whosoever will be great among you, shall be your minister:*
44 *And whosoever of you will be the chiefest, shall be servant of all.*

45 For even the Son of man came not to be ministered unto, but to minister, and to give his life a ransom for many.

Jesus illustrated a great example of humility in service when He girded Himself with a towel and washed the feet of His disciples (John 13:4–15). The Son of God humbled Himself as the lowliest of servants to perform a menial task. Jesus effectively used the most powerful method of teaching—teaching by example. He demonstrated the humility He expected of His disciples.

Luke 14:11

11 For whosoever exalteth himself shall be abased; and he that humbleth himself shall be exalted.

Here we see a promise to a servant who exhibits this quality of humility: he will be rewarded. How can we show our humility as a servant of the Lord Jesus Christ?

Humility is shown by gratefulness. A humble servant is a grateful servant. One common lament about young people today is that they are not grateful. We make a special effort at our church to encourage our young people to have a good testimony for Christ by teaching them to have an "attitude of gratitude." But we first need to set the example ourselves.

As servants of the Lord Jesus Christ, one of the most important attributes of our lives should be that of gratitude. We are commanded to be thankful.

1 Thessalonians 5:18

18 In every thing give thanks: for this is the will of God in Christ Jesus concerning you.

Would you like to know the will of God for your life? Part of God's will for your life is to give God thanks *in everything*—not just in pleasant times, but in hard and confusing times as well. He is worthy of our gratitude.

Have you ever stopped to think that *anything* God gives us is better than we deserve? If God gave us what we really deserve, where would we be? The wages of sin (and all have sinned) is what? (See Romans 6:23.) Death! This is not just a physical death, but a spiritual death. Certainly, we need to be grateful for the mercy of God.

D. Joyful

The Bible has much to say about the joy that a believer can and should have in Christ.

- Joy for the birth of Christ

  Luke 2:10–11

  10 *And the angel said unto them, Fear not: for, behold, I bring you* ***good tidings of great joy,*** *which shall be to all people.*
  11 *For unto you is born this day in the city of David a Saviour, which is Christ the Lord.*

- Joy for the Word of God

  1 Thessalonians 1:6

  6 *And ye became followers of us, and of the Lord, having received the word in much affliction, with joy of the Holy Ghost.*

- Joy in God's presence

  Psalm 16:11

  11 *Thou wilt shew me the path of life: in thy presence is fulness of joy; at thy right hand there are pleasures for evermore.*

Psalm 100 says, *"Serve the Lord with gladness"* (verse 2). A servant of the Lord should serve joyfully. Why? Because *"the Lord is good; his mercy is everlasting; and his truth endureth to all generations"* (verse 5).

So far, we have discussed what a servant of the Lord is supposed to *be*. Now we'll talk about what a servant is supposed to *do*, but we need to realize this: If we are what we are supposed to be, we will do what we are supposed to do.

II. Outward Qualities of a Servant of the Lord

A. *Obedient in his actions*

A servant is to execute the commands and the wishes of his master. He must obey his master, or he is no servant at all.

Luke 17:7–10

7 But which of you, having a servant plowing or feeding cattle, will say unto him by and by, when he is come from the field, Go and sit down to meat?

8 And will not rather say unto him, Make ready wherewith I may sup, and gird thyself, and serve me, till I have eaten and drunken; and afterward thou shalt eat and drink?

9 Doth he thank that servant because he did the things that were commanded him? I trow [think] not.

10 So likewise ye, when ye shall have done all those things which are commanded you, say, We are unprofitable servants: we have done that which was our duty to do.

A servant is to obey his master and not count it a remarkable thing. He is not to desire or expect special praise because he did as he was told. His duty is whatever his master commands. In fact, the servant is to count himself as *unprofitable* (in the Greek, this word means "useless, good for nothing") if he only does his duty. The servant must give one hundred percent obedience to his master.

1 Peter 2:18
18 Servants, be subject to your masters with all fear; not only to the good and gentle, but also to the froward.

The word *froward* here means "unfair" or "surly," "perverse" or "wicked." Its very definition is the antithesis of "good and gentle." So the obedience the servant must render his master does not depend on the disposition of the master, or on how the servant feels toward the master. The servant is supposed to obey an unkind master as well as a kind master.

Titus 2:9
9 Exhort servants to be obedient unto their own masters, and to please them well in all things; not answering again.

In other words, the servant is to obediently please the master in all things without putting up any arguments. To put it bluntly, as your parents may have told you when you were young and tended to be a little rebellious, "Keep your mouth shut, and do what you're told."

Let's return to the thought of the *unprofitable servant*: If one hundred percent obedience is unprofitable, then how can a servant become profitable? How can we give more than one hundred percent? We can go the "second mile" that Jesus described in the Sermon on the Mount.

Matthew 5:41
41 *And whosoever shall compel thee to go a mile, go with him twain.*

So if we are required to go a mile, we ought to be willing to go two miles.

Illustration

Ernie Banks played for the Chicago Cubs and earned the right to appear in the Baseball Hall of Fame. Known as "Mr. Cub," he is one of the most beloved figures in Chicago sports history. His statistics are impressive, but what Chicago loved most about Ernie Banks was his attitude toward the game. Ernie Banks used to say, "Let's play two today." Double-headers are a rarity nowadays—two games for the price of one? But years ago, ball clubs used to play two games several times per season. Ernie Banks would have done it every day if they would let him. "Let's play two today." You want me to go a mile? Let's go two!

Enthusiastic obedience transforms us into profitable servants.

Illustration

One duty of a music leader is to lead the congregational singing. If he were to approach the pulpit at the beginning of the service with a blank expression on his face and greet the congregation in a monotone voice asking them to sing with him, he would be obeying the basic requirements of the position—he is leading the singing—but much more is needed. A song leader needs to generate enthusiasm, and he does that in part by being enthusiastic himself. He needs more than obedience; he needs enthusiastic obedience!

Enthusiasm makes a difference. Real enthusiasm comes from within. It is not something you put on to look good to others temporarily. If our enthusiasm is only a façade, it is essentially useless.

Illustration

Hollywood actors, for the most part, are very different from the characters they portray. They are paid an incredible amount of money to pretend that they are somebody else. For example, John Wayne's real name was Marion Morrison, and he was born in Iowa. He was not a real cowboy and never served in the military. He was only a prop boy in a studio when somebody noticed him and decided to try him as an actor.

So when it comes to enthusiasm, don't just be an actor. The Greek word *entheos* from which we get our word *enthusiasm* means "having the god within." As believers, we have God in us! Therefore, the source of our enthusiasm is the indwelling Holy Spirit. As we allow the Holy Spirit free reign in our lives, our enthusiasm will show, and it will be genuine.

We need to obey the Lord with the enthusiasm that comes from the consciousness of His presence within us. Enthusiasm makes obedience much more effective. Obeying with cheerfulness also makes a difference in your attitude toward serving the Lord, and it will affect others as well. Enthusiasm is contagious!

TEACHING TIP

Anyone who invests in the lives of children knows the value of obedience. Wise parents and teachers spend much time emphasizing and training in obedience. When a child obeys with a good attitude and enthusiasm, the parent or teacher is encouraged.

Share an example (from your own or your children's life) when obeying cheerfully made a difference. If time allows, ask for a few other testimonies as well.

We spoke earlier of being whole-hearted, but let's revisit it briefly in this context. There is half-hearted obedience, and there is whole-hearted obedience. The actions may be the same, temporarily, but the results will be very different in the end. Half-hearted obedience will falter and will eventually become disobedience. Whole-hearted obedience is what the Lord desires from His servants.

Colossians 3:22–24

22 *Servants, obey in all things your masters according to the flesh; not with eyeservice, as menpleasers; but in singleness of heart, fearing God:*
23 *And whatsoever ye do, do it heartily, as to the Lord, and not unto men;*
24 *Knowing that of the Lord ye shall receive the reward of the inheritance: for ye serve the Lord Christ.*

This word *heartily* in the King James Version is usually translated "soul." Remember that Jesus said, "*Thou shalt love the Lord thy God with* ***all thy heart,*** *and with* ***all thy soul,*** *and with* ***all thy mind****...Thou shalt love thy neighbour as thyself*" (Matthew 22:37, 39).

Obey God, yes, but don't be content with bare-bones obedience. Serve the Lord with enthusiasm and with all of your heart. Let it show!

B. Diligent in his duties

A diligent person is one who is hard working, industrious, conscientious, and thorough—a person who does his best. The Lord certainly gave us His best when He gave us His Son. Should we not be willing to give Him our best in return?

Nehemiah provided a stellar example of diligence. When we first encounter Nehemiah, he was a servant, the cupbearer to the king of Persia. This was a very important post. The *International Standard Bible Encyclopedia* says this:

> **Cupbearer**: An officer of high rank at ancient oriental courts, whose duty it was to serve the wine at the king's table. Because of the constant fear of plots and intrigues, a person must be regarded as thoroughly trustworthy to hold this position. He must guard against poison in the king's cup, and was sometimes required to swallow some of the wine before serving it. His confidential relations with the king often endeared him to his sovereign and also gave him a position of great influence.

Nehemiah was a diligent servant, and when released from captivity to rebuild the wall around the city, he led his people to be diligent as well. They had to be diligent because the enemies of God and of God's people surrounded them on every side, trying every way they could to stop the work. Those who were building the wall kept their weapons ready to fight for their lives at any moment.

In spite of all opposition and difficulties, the wall was completed in just fifty-two days. In Nehemiah 4:6, we see one of the reasons for success: "*…the people had a mind to work.*" That word for *mind* is more often translated "heart." Because the people had a mind and a heart to work—because they were diligent—they accomplished a great work for God.

The diligence Christ deserves is emphasized in a hymn by S.C. Kirk and Grant Tullar:

> Hear ye the Master's call, "Give Me thy best!"
> For, be it great or small, that is His test.
> Do then the best you can, not for reward,
> Not for the praise of men, but for the Lord.
>
> Every work for Jesus will be blest,
> But He asks from everyone his best.
> Our talents may be few, these may be small,
> But unto Him is due our best, our all.

Employers have a right to expect that their employees will do their best. We as Christian believers who want to have a good testimony for the Lord, need to be diligent at our places of employment. (In times of a lean economy especially, if we are not willing to work hard and do our best, it wouldn't be too difficult for almost any employer to find several other people who are willing. Diligence can make a difference.) Be diligent in every duty the Lord entrusts to your care—in the workplace, at home, or in ministry.

C. *Faithful in his responsibilities*

1 Corinthians 4:2

2 *Moreover it is required in stewards, that a man be found faithful.*

In the parable of the nobleman and his three stewards (Matthew 25:14–21), we learn that, above all else, God desires for His servants to be faithful. From beginning to end, the Bible stresses faithfulness. The individuals whom God has blessed and used throughout history have all had one thing in common: they have been faithful. We can all be faithful, no matter what our different abilities or backgrounds may be.

Consider these three important aspects of faithfulness:

- *Faithfulness is required* (1 Corinthians 4:2).
  It's not what we have that is important, but rather it is what we do with what we have.

- *Faithfulness is reckoned* (Romans 14:10).
  Our works will be compared, not against others' works, but against what we could have accomplished.

- *Faithfulness will be rewarded* (Matthew 6:4, 16:27; 1 Corinthians 3:13–14).
  Of all of the things the Lord could say about our lives, will He be able to say that we have been faithful?

Conclusion

A true servant of the Lord must have these qualities of wholeheartedness, humility, obedience, diligence, and faithfulness. Christ deserves our best in each of these areas. A simple question: Are we the servants that our Master deserves?

Study Questions

1. What are two specific characteristics that we need in order to serve God whole-heartedly?
   We must serve with loyalty and love.

2. Christ is the greatest example of humility. What are three ways you can think of in which He demonstrated humility?
   Answers will vary but may include the following: He washed His disciples' feet; He ate with publicans and sinners; He willingly submitted to the humiliation of the Cross.

3. What three outward qualities given in this lesson should mark a servant of the Lord?
   A servant of the Lord should be obedient in his actions, diligent in his duties, and faithful in his responsibilities.

4. A servant who only does what he is told is an "unprofitable" servant. How can a servant give more than one hundred percent?
   He can go the "second mile" and serve with enthusiastic obedience.

5. People serve for a variety of reasons—some pure and others selfish. List some possible motives for service (both good and bad). What words in your list describes your motives?
   Answers will vary but may include the following: love, gratitude, humility, payment, appreciation, public notice, etc.

6. An effective servant of the Lord serves whole-heartedly. Would those who know you best be able to honestly say that you love the Lord with all your heart and give Him your all?
   Answers will vary.

7. On a scale of one to ten, where would you rate your enthusiasm for obediently serving the Lord?
   Answers will vary.

8. The most needful quality of a servant is faithfulness. In what ways can you grow in faithfulness to the Lord, your family, or your church?
   Answers will vary.

Memory Verse

1 Samuel 12:24

24 Only fear the Lord, and serve him in truth with all your heart: for consider how great things he hath done for you.

LESSON ELEVEN

A Friend to Others

Text

JOHN 15:13
13 Greater love hath no man than this, that a man lay down his life for his friends.

Overview

God has allowed us to build relationships with others to sharpen, encourage, and challenge one another to walk closer to Him and fulfill His purpose for our lives. Wisely use the influence you have, however small you think it to be, to be a godly friend to others.

Lesson Theme

A true friend is a precious treasure, and we have the opportunity to be that true friend for others. Jesus Himself is our greatest, most faithful Friend. When we extend His love to others, we can help our friends grow in their relationship with the Lord.

Lesson Objectives

At the conclusion of the lesson, each student should:

1. Look for ways to encourage and edify their friends to accomplish God's purpose for their lives.

2. Commit to being faithful to their friends, even during times of difficulty and discouragement or when faithfulness requires rebuke.
3. Offer forgiveness to friends who have wronged them.

Teaching Outline

Introduction

I. A Friend is Encouraging and Edifying
   A. Encouraging
   B. Edifying

II. A Friend Goes the Second Mile
   A. Fills needs
   B. Patient

III. A Friend is Faithful

IV. A Friend is Forgiving

Conclusion

LESSON ELEVEN

A Friend to Others

Text

John 15:13

13 *Greater love hath no man than this, that a man lay down his life for his friends.*

Introduction

A true friend is a precious treasure, and we have the opportunity to *be* that true friend for others. Jesus Himself is our greatest, most faithful Friend. When we extend His love to others, we help our friends grow in their relationship with the Lord.

In training young people, we often emphasize the need to avoid "the wrong crowd" because we know the power of a friend's influence. Our closest friends should be wisely chosen as they need to be ones who sharpen us spiritually.

Yet we also must be very conscious of the influence we have over our friends. Are *we* the right kind of friends?

I. A Friend Is Encouraging and Edifying

A true friend will:

- lift you up—not tear you down
- help—not hurt
- encourage—not discourage
- edify—not diminish

In essence, a true friend will help you become more of what you need to be rather than pulling you in the wrong direction.

A. Encouraging

The word *encourage* means "to inspire with hope, courage, or confidence; hearten." (*The American Heritage Dictionary of the English Language*, Third Edition Copyright ©1992 by Houghton Mifflin Company. Electronic version.) We have all had low times in our lives when we needed encouragement, inspiration, and a reason to keep going. Others need encouragement from us as well. How can we be a friend who encourages?

One of the greatest tools to build up others is encouraging words. The Bible says, "*A word fitly spoken is like apples of gold in pictures of silver*" (Proverbs 25:11). Proverbs 15:23 underscores this truth when it says "*a word spoken in due season, how good is it!*" An encouraging word from a friend can make such a difference.

Illustration

A young freshman-to-be arrived at college, having traveled a long way from home. In his assigned room, he saw that his roommates had all checked in, and every bed had already been claimed, leaving just a small couch. Feeling exhausted and excluded, he was ready to turn around and go home.

Just then, one of his roommates, an upperclassman, came in and introduced himself. Recognizing the dilemma of the poor forlorn freshman, the upperclassman offered his friendship and his bunk. The freshman not only stayed, he eventually graduated, and more than thirty years later he is still serving God. The course of a life may have been changed by just a word of encouragement. Even more importantly, one word of encouragement early in life enabled him to encourage others many years later.

Wouldn't you like to be the one who takes the time to encourage someone today? It could make a great deal of difference!

The Bible records several instances when people, even godly leaders, needed encouragement.

Moses needed encouragement. In a battle between Israel and Amalek, God used the support of Moses' friends to make the difference.

Exodus 17:9–12

9 *And Moses said unto Joshua, Choose us out men, and go out, fight with Amalek: to morrow I will stand on the top of the hill with the rod of God in mine hand.*

10 *So Joshua did as Moses had said to him, and fought with Amalek: and Moses, Aaron, and Hur went up to the top of the hill.*

11 *And it came to pass, when Moses held up his hand, that Israel prevailed: and when he let down his hand, Amalek prevailed.*
12 *But Moses' hands were heavy; and they took a stone, and put it under him, and he sat thereon; and Aaron and Hur stayed up his hands, the one on the one side, and the other on the other side; and his hands were steady until the going down of the sun.*

As the battle waged, Moses wearied as he held up his hands to invoke the blessing of God. Aaron and Hur "*stayed up his hands*"—held up his hands, supported him. The Bible says that "*his hands were steady until the going down of the sun.*" Moses' friends encouraged him with their support.

David needed encouragement. Saul, the king of Israel, was determined to wipe out his competition for the throne, so David ran for his life. But Jonathan, Saul's firstborn son, loved David "*as his own soul*" (1 Samuel 18:1). Jonathan had the right to be the next king, but he decided that he was going to be a friend to David. In 1 Samuel 23:16, we read that Jonathan went to David and "*strengthened his hand in God.*" Many times there is no better gift you can give your friend than the encouragement that strengthens his hand in God.

The disciples needed encouragement. Jesus' disciples experienced a wide gamut of emotions as they followed Christ. Jesus often used His words to encourage them in God's faithfulness and love for them.

JOHN 14:1

1 *Let not your heart be troubled: ye believe in God, believe also in me.*

Luke 12:6–7

6 *Are not five sparrows sold for two farthings, and not one of them is forgotten before God?*
7 *But even the very hairs of your head are all numbered. Fear not therefore: ye are of more value than many sparrows.*

Matthew 7:7–8

7 *Ask, and it shall be given you; seek, and ye shall find; knock, and it shall be opened unto you:*
8 *For every one that asketh receiveth; and he that seeketh findeth; and to him that knocketh it shall be opened.*

Jesus needed encouragement. Hours before sacrificing His life at Calvary, Jesus agonized in prayer in the Garden of Gethsemane. He prayed so earnestly that "*his sweat was as it were great drops of blood falling down to the ground*" (Luke 22:44). It was then that "*there appeared an angel unto him from heaven, strengthening him*" (Luke 22:43).

Determine to be a friend who is an encourager. Look for those who may need your encouragement, and speak up with an encouraging word to someone today.

B. *Edifying*

The word *edify* means "to instruct especially so as to encourage intellectual, moral, or spiritual improvement." (*The American Heritage Dictionary of the English Language*, Third Edition Copyright ©1992 by Houghton Mifflin Company. Electronic version.) The word *edify* comes from a Latin word meaning "to build." (Compare to the word *edifice,* which means "a building.") We need to allow God to use us to build our friends into what He would have them be and to help them in their intellectual, moral, and spiritual growth.

Illustration

William Wilberforce (1759–1833), one of the most prominent figures in English history, fought for the abolition of the slave trade in the British Empire for twenty years. His abolition bill was defeated time after time, often by narrow margins and sometimes by dirty political tricks. His lifelong friend John Newton, a former slave trader who had become a bold Christian (author of the hymn "Amazing Grace"), gave words of edification to Wilberforce during a time when he was in great despair.

Newton reminded Wilberforce of the story of Daniel—a public man like Wilberforce, who trusted in God, was faithful to his duty, and saw God deliver him from his enemies. "The God whom you serve continually," Newton told him, quoting King Darius' words to Daniel in the lion's den, "is able to preserve and deliver you. He will see you through." Not only did Newton succeed in encouraging his friend, he edified him by sharing the Word of God with him and helping him to grow in his faith.

Illustration

The book of Esther in Scripture is a thrilling account of God's sovereignty to care for His people and the winsome courage displayed by Esther. After Haman tricked the king into ordering the destruction of all the Jews, God used Esther to turn the king's heart to reverse the sentence, allowing the Jews to destroy their enemies—including Haman. Esther's bravery might never have been shown had it not been for her older cousin Mordecai's words of encouragement and edification.

Esther 4:13–14

13 *Then Mordecai commanded to answer Esther, Think not with thyself that thou shalt escape in the king's house, more than all the Jews.*

14 *For if thou altogether holdest thy peace at this time, then shall there enlargement and deliverance arise to the Jews from another place; but thou and thy father's house shall be destroyed: and who knoweth whether thou art come to the kingdom for such a time as this?*

When Esther thought the task before her was impossible, Mordecai pointed her to a great spiritual principle—the great purpose of God in bringing her to that place at that time.

A godly friend has the power to increase the effectiveness of another through words of edification.

Proverbs 27:17

17 *Iron sharpeneth iron; so a man sharpeneth the countenance of his friend.*

Sharpening a knife or a saw increases its effectiveness. One of the best things you can do for a friend is to help him become a better person—intellectually, morally, and spiritually.

Proverbs 27:9

9 *Ointment and perfume rejoice the heart: so doth the sweetness of a man's friend by hearty counsel.*

Christ consistently edified His disciples through His example, His words, and His works. His purpose was for them to carry on the work of God in the power of the Holy Spirit after He ascended to His Father. His goal, always, was to help them grow.

Second Peter 3:18 admonishes us to *"grow in grace, and in the knowledge of our Lord and Saviour Jesus Christ."* A true friend will do whatever he can to assist in that growth process. Do your friends help you grow in the Lord? Are you a friend who helps others grow?

II. A Friend Goes the Second Mile

Friendship goes beyond the call of duty and volunteers for unrequired service. We call this "going the second mile." In Matthew 5:41, Jesus said, *"And whosoever shall compel thee to go a mile, go with him twain."* In other words, go beyond what is expected; do more than just what is required.

COMMENTARY

The word translated shall compel, *is of Persian origin. Post offices were then unknown. In order that the royal commands might be delivered with safety and dispatched in different parts of the empire, Cyrus stationed horsemen at proper intervals on all the great public highways. One of those delivered the message to another, and intelligence was thus rapidly and safely communicated. These heralds were permitted to compel any person, or to press any horse, boat, ship, or other vehicle into service that they might need, for the quick transmission of the king's commandments. It was to this custom that our Saviour refers. Rather, says he, than resist a public authority, requiring your attendance and aid for a certain distance, go peaceably twice the distance.*
—Barnes' New Testament Notes

A. *Fills needs*

Friendship and love are not just feelings but a willingness to meet others' needs. Notice these Bible examples of men who met the needs of others:

The Good Samaritan met his neighbor's needs (Luke 10:30–37). A man was robbed, beaten, and left for dead by the highway. A priest came by, and "*when he saw him, he passed by on the other side.*" "Poor guy," he may have said to himself, "that's what happens when you hang around the wrong kind of people. I hope he's learned his lesson." Then a Levite came along, "*looked on him, and passed by on the other side.*" "Poor guy," he may have said to himself, "he looks unclean, with all that blood. I hope somebody comes along and takes care of him." We don't really know what was going through their minds, but the Bible says that they saw the man in need, avoided him, and kept on their way.

Later a Samaritan passed by, and the Bible says that, "*when he saw him, he had compassion on him, And went to him, and bound up his wounds, pouring in oil and wine, and set him on his own beast, and brought him to an inn, and took care of him. And on the morrow when he departed, he took out two pence, and gave them to the host, and said unto him, Take care of him; and whatsoever thou spendest more, when I come again, I will repay thee.*"

The priest, the Levite, and the Samaritan all saw the man in need, but only the Samaritan—who could have spent all of his time dwelling on the injustice and discrimination he encountered in his own life—actually fulfilled the needs of the wounded man. The Samaritan probably did not even know this wounded man, but, truly, he was a friend to him.

Jonathan met David's needs (1 Samuel 20:27–34). Jonathan was King Saul's son—next in line for the throne. Yet Jonathan knew God had chosen David to replace Saul as king, and Jonathan loved David. When Saul attempted to kill David, Jonathan risked his own life to warn David of the danger and help him escape.

Jesus Christ meets our needs. The best friend we have is Jesus Christ. He meets our every need—physical, emotional, and spiritual. As Joseph Scriven so aptly wrote, "What a Friend we have in Jesus!"

To be a second-mile friend, we need to look for the needs of our friends and do whatever we can to fill them—even before we're asked. How far are you willing to go in meeting the needs of your friends?

B. Patient

A second-mile friend is longsuffering—he is patient, persevering, and does not give up.

Think of Jesus again, with all of the patience and longsuffering He exhibited toward His disciples. Time and time again, they disappointed Him with their stubbornness, their ignorance, and their lack of faith. He rebuked them, but He never gave up on them.

And how patient He is with us! We all have great need of His patience. First John 1:9 promises that as long as we keep confessing our sin, He keeps forgiving: "*If we confess our sins, he is faithful and just to forgive us our sins, and to cleanse us from all unrighteousness.*" Lamentations 3:22 records a brilliant promise of the Lord's patience: "*It is of the Lord's mercies that we are not consumed, because his compassions fail not.*"

Like a potter who patiently shapes and reshapes his clay, the Lord is patient in His dealings with us.

Isaiah 64:8

8 *But now, O Lord, thou art our father; we are the clay, and thou our potter; and we all are the work of thy hand.*

Jeremiah 18:1–6

1 *The word which came to Jeremiah from the Lord, saying,*
2 *Arise, and go down to the potter's house, and there I will cause thee to hear my words.*
3 *Then I went down to the potter's house, and, behold, he wrought a work on the wheels.*
4 *And the vessel that he made of clay was marred in the hand of the potter: so he made it again another vessel, as seemed good to the potter to make it.*
5 *Then the word of the Lord came to me, saying,*
6 *O house of Israel, cannot I do with you as this potter? saith the Lord. Behold, as the clay is in the potter's hand, so are ye in mine hand, O house of Israel.*

The potter had a purpose in mind for the clay, and though the clay was not always cooperative, the potter didn't throw it away.

One outstanding characteristic of a workman, artist, or craftsman is patience. It takes much time and painstaking effort to make something that is truly worthwhile and valuable.

The artist Michelangelo worked for four years to paint the frescoes on the ceiling of the Sistine Chapel. The mighty sculptures on Mount Rushmore were carved over a period of fourteen years. The Washington Monument was finally completed some thirty-six years after construction began.

How foolish it would have been for the financers or workmen on these projects to give up after just a couple of years. Today, these works of art are a testimony to the patience required in their design and construction.

Our own lives, as well, are a testimony to God's patience with us. He is working in each of our lives individually and specifically. When we begin to feel frustrated with our friends, we must remember God's patience toward us. All of us could wear the plea I read on a bumper sticker: "Be patient; God isn't finished with me yet!" All of us are still "under construction." You could be the friend that has the patience to encourage another on to greater growth.

III. A Friend Is Faithful

A faithful friend is an incredible gift. To be a faithful friend is an incredible task.

Proverbs 17:17

17 ***A friend loveth at all times,*** *and a brother is born for adversity.*

In times of prosperity or poverty, in times of joy or sorrow, in times of health or illness, a true friend will remain faithful.

Proverbs 27:10

10 ***Thine own friend, and thy father's friend, forsake not;*** *neither go into thy brother's house in the day of thy calamity…*

Silvanus is a biblical example of a faithful friend. Peter even specifically referred to this man as *"a faithful brother unto you"* (1 Peter 5:12). The name Silvanus is the long form of the name Silas; quite possibly this is the same man who was imprisoned with the Apostle Paul in Philippi (Acts 16).

Certainly Silas was a faithful friend, willing to share Paul's persecution and shame for the preaching of the Gospel. Paul and Silas shared in troubles (including a public whipping and imprisonment), but they also shared in the miraculous deliverance of God. What would Silas have missed had he not been a faithful friend?

We've already seen David and Jonathan's friendship in relation to encouragement and meeting needs, but notice the incredible faithfulness these two men demonstrated toward each other—right up to the end of their lives. Jonathan was David's friend even when it cost him the favor of his own father and the throne. He remained faithful and loyal until the end of his life when he died on the battlefield (1 Samuel 31:2). David consistently honored Jonathan's memory (2 Samuel 1:25–27), and after Jonathan's death, David cared for his son, Mephibosheth (2 Samuel 9:1–13). David and Jonathan's reunion in Heaven must have been a special thing to see.

Sometimes faithfulness involves being willing to rebuke a friend for his own good.

TEACHING TIP

Share a personal illustration of a friend who has demonstrated faithfulness to you. Describe in what ways he/she communicated loyalty to you during a discouraging time in your life.

Proverbs 27:6

6 *Faithful are the wounds of a friend; but the kisses of an enemy are deceitful"*

If your friend is headed in the wrong direction, a direction contrary to God, you ought to do what is necessary to help him back on the right path. It may not be pleasant to faithfully, honestly, and lovingly confront another, but the rewards are tremendous later.

When David committed the sins of adultery and murder, the prophet Nathan courageously confronted David with the truth (2 Samuel 12:1–15). God used the faithfulness of Nathan to bring David to repentance and restoration. Later, David named a son after his faithful friend Nathan (1 Chronicles 3:5).

IV. A Friend Is Forgiving

Who hasn't needed forgiveness from his friends? We so easily wound our friends with thoughtless words or careless deeds, and we appreciate it when our friends extend forgiveness to us. We need to learn to also demonstrate a forgiving spirit to others.

Our Lord Jesus Christ is the greatest example of forgiving His friends. During His darkest hour, His disciples all forsook Him and fled (Matthew 26:56; Mark 14:50). Peter denied Him three times with increasing indignation (Matthew 26:69–75). Only John is mentioned as being present at the Cross (John 19:26–27).

But witness the tender scene when Jesus appeared to His disciples after His Resurrection (John 20:19–29). He said to them, "*Peace be unto you,*" and showed them His hands and His side. "*Then were the disciples glad, when they saw the Lord,*" in part because they knew the Lord in His mercy had forgiven them. He was even gentle and forgiving with Thomas, who refused to believe Christ had resurrected until he saw for himself. Could any of our friends treat us as badly as Jesus' friends treated Him? Still, Jesus forgave it all.

In fact, if we insist on being unforgiving and holding grudges, we will not be forgiven ourselves.

Matthew 6:14–15
14 *For if ye forgive men their trespasses, your heavenly Father will also forgive you:*
15 *But if ye forgive not men their trespasses, neither will your Father forgive your trespasses.*

Charles Spurgeon had this to say: "Very sweet is it to pass by other men's offenses against ourselves, for thus we learn how sweet it is to the Lord to pardon us." [Source: *Popular Exposition of Matthew*]

COMMENTARY

We must forgive, as we hope to be forgiven; and therefore must not only bear no malice, nor mediate revenge, but must not upbraid our brother with the injuries he has done us, nor rejoice in any hurt that befalls him, but must be ready to help him and do him good, and if he repent and desire to be friends again, we must be free and familiar with him, as before.—Matthew Henry's Bible Commentary

Peter asked Jesus, *"Lord, how oft shall my brother sin against me, and I forgive him? till seven times?"* (Matthew 18:21). Instead of justifying Peter's unforgiving attitude, Jesus answered, *"I say not unto thee, Until seven times: but, Until seventy times seven."* This term, "seventy times seven," basically represents infinity. Even taking the term literally, by the time you've done something 490 times, you might as well make it permanent!

Not only did Jesus forgive His friends, He also forgave His enemies. Even as He was on the Cross, He prayed for those crucifying Him: "*Father, forgive them; for they know not what they do*" (Luke 23:34).

Matthew 5:44–48

44 *But I say unto you, Love your enemies, bless them that curse you, do good to them that hate you, and pray for them which despitefully use you, and persecute you;*
45 *That ye may be the children of your Father which is in heaven: for he maketh his sun to rise on the evil and on the good, and sendeth rain on the just and on the unjust.*
46 *For if ye love them which love you, what reward have ye? do not even the publicans the same?*
47 *And if ye salute your brethren only, what do ye more than others? do not even the publicans so?*
48 *Be ye therefore perfect, even as your Father which is in heaven is perfect.*

A friend is forgiving, even to those who don't really deserve it! Do any of us really *deserve* forgiveness? No. It is when we consider the forgiveness that Christ has freely given to us that we see our responsibility to forgive others. "*And be ye kind one to another, tenderhearted, forgiving one another, even as God for Christ's sake hath forgiven you*" (Ephesians 4:32).

Conclusion

God has allowed us to build relationships with others to sharpen, encourage, and challenge one another to walk closer to Him and fulfill His purpose for our lives. Wisely use the influence you have, however small you think it to be, to be a godly friend to others. Also, place godly influences in your own life by choosing godly friends.

Never forget the example of Jesus Christ we have right before us in the Word of God. What a Friend!

Study Questions

1. How did Aaron and Hur encourage Moses during battle?
   They "stayed up his hands." They supported him.

2. In what two ways can a friend go the second mile?
   A friend can go the second mile by meeting other's needs and demonstrating longsuffering (patience).

3. In what ways did Jonathan's friendship with David cost him?
   It cost him favor with his father and the throne.

4. What numerical value does the term "seventy times seven" represent?
   "Seventy times seven" represents infinity.

5. Relate a time when someone encouraged you during a difficult time or task. What did they do that encouraged you, and how can you show similar encouragement to another?
   Answers will vary but may include the following: they believed in me; they offered assistance; they wrote a note of thanks; they shared Scripture.

6. Is there a current relationship you have that could benefit from your growth in longsuffering? Write down at least two ways you could exercise patience with this person.
   Answers will vary.

7. Are any of your friends going through a difficult season and needing a friend's faithfulness? How could you remind your friend(s) of your commitment to them this week?
Answers will vary but may include the following: a note of encouragement, spending some time with them—perhaps over a sandwich, specific prayer for/with them, etc.

8. Friends carry a tremendous weight of influence on one another. How are you using the influence you carry to encourage your friends to love the Lord more and walk closer to Him? What could you do this week to use your influence for God?
Answers will vary.

Memory Verse

John 15:13

13 *Greater love hath no man than this, that a man lay down his life for his friends.*

LESSON TWELVE

A Child of the Heavenly Father

Text

GALATIANS 4:5–7

5 *To redeem them that were under the law, that we might receive the adoption of sons.*

6 *And because ye are sons, God hath sent forth the Spirit of his Son into your hearts, crying, Abba, Father.*

7 *Wherefore thou art no more a servant, but a son; and if a son, then an heir of God through Christ.*

Overview

The sweetest relationship we have with God is that He is our Father, and we are His children. Children are very precious, and their relationship with their parents is one of sacrificial and unending love. God's love and protection of His children is also unending and of infinite proportions.

Lesson Theme

Somewhere in the salutation of nearly all of Paul's epistles he mentions *"God our Father."* No matter what may have been the main subject of the letter, Paul wanted the believers to know, first of all, that God was their Father. Living in the light of that close relationship with the Lord allows everything else to fall into place. We must strive to be the right kind of children in order to be the fulfilled Christians God wants us to be.

Lesson Objectives

At the conclusion of the lesson, each student should:

1. Know how to become a child of God by being born again.
2. Understand benefits of being a child of God.
3. Commit themselves to be obedient and faithful to the Heavenly Father.

Teaching Outline

Introduction

I. Becoming God's Child
   - A. God wants everyone to be His child.
   - B. God will never disinherit a family member.

II. Benefits of Being God's Child
   - A. Family name
   - B. Inheritance
   - C. Home
   - D. Protection

III. Being the Right Kind of Child
   - A. Obedience
   - B. Faithfulness

Conclusion

LESSON TWELVE

A Child of the Heavenly Father

Text

GALATIANS 4:5–7

5 *To redeem them that were under the law, that we might receive the adoption of sons.*

6 *And because ye are sons, God hath sent forth the Spirit of his Son into your hearts, crying, Abba, Father.*

7 *Wherefore thou art no more a servant, but a son; and if a son, then an heir of God through Christ.*

Introduction

Of our various relationships to God, we now address the sweetest of all—we are children of God. Those fortunate enough to be parents know how precious children are. There is nothing we would not do for our children—no sacrifice is too great. Their joy is our joy; their pain is our pain. And yet, we cannot even touch the loving care and concern that God has for His children, for His love is far greater than ours.

God considers children one of His richest blessings.

PSALM 127:3

3 Lo, children are an heritage of the LORD: and the fruit of the womb is his reward.

In Old Testament days, one of the greatest blessings for a man was to have many children and descendants. God promised Abram, whose name He changed to Abraham, that He would make of him a great nation (Genesis 12:2). The name *Abraham* actually means "father of many nations." (Genesis 17:5). God told Abraham, *"And I will make thee exceeding fruitful, and I will make nations of thee, and kings shall come out of thee"* (Genesis 17:6).

Of the Bible's many genealogies, the most important is the earthly genealogy of the Lord Jesus Christ (Matthew 1:1–17; Luke 3:23–38). Have you ever considered what a miracle it is that an unbroken line of sons should continue for so many centuries? Consider, for example, that today, a mere two hundred years after the birth of Abraham Lincoln, he has no direct descendants living today. It was extremely vital for a Jew to be able to trace his lineage. An established lineage was a matter of legality as well as family pride.

The Apostle John expressed his high regard for a man named Gaius, who seems to have been one of his converts. In an epistle to Gaius, John wrote, *"I have no greater joy than to hear that my children walk in truth"* (3 John 4). The Apostle John lived a long and prosperous life for the Lord, and he found that his greatest happiness was when his spiritual children lived in obedience to the Word of God.

We can make our Heavenly Father happy and give Him joy when we walk in His truth and live our lives in obedience to Him.

Let's look at both our blessings and our responsibilities as a child of God.

I. Becoming God's Child

How do you become a child of God? In John 3, a Pharisee named Nicodemus came to Jesus by night and asked Him that question. Nicodemus knew Jesus was a teacher from God because nobody could have done the miracles that Jesus did unless God was with him. Jesus answered Nicodemus, "*Verily, verily, I say unto thee, Except a man be born again, he cannot see the kingdom of God*" (John 3:3). We become a child of our parents through a *physical* birth, and we become a child of God through a *spiritual* birth. By receiving God's gift of salvation, we are "*born again*" into the family of God.

To be born again, one must understand the following:

- All of us are sinners and are condemned before God (Romans 3:23, 5:12, 6:23).
- Christ died for our sins (Romans 5:8).
- We must trust Christ for salvation (Romans 10:9–10, 13).

TEACHING TIP

If you have students whom you are not sure are saved, this would be an excellent opportunity to give them a clear Gospel presentation. As a class, look up each of the verses in the bullet points above. You can then explain their significance to the statement before them in this lesson. Encourage your students to trust Christ as their Saviour.

A. *God wants everyone to be His child.*

God wants everyone, every single human being, to be His child.

John 3:16

16 *For God so loved the world, that he gave his only begotten Son, that* **whosoever** *believeth in him should not perish, but have everlasting life.*

Jesus left nobody out when He died on the Cross; the invitation for salvation is open to all.

2 Corinthians 5:15

15 *And that* **he died for all,** *that they which live should not henceforth live unto themselves, but unto him which died for them, and rose again.*

Romans 10:13

13 *For* **whosoever** *shall call upon the name of the Lord shall be saved.*

God's will is that all people receive His gift of eternal life and become His children. Many people do reject the Saviour, but that is against His will. Second Peter 3:9 explains that God is "*not willing that any should perish, but that all should come to repentance.*" He invites everyone, and everyone is individually responsible to either accept or reject the invitation. The Bible says, "*But* ***as many as received him,*** *to them gave he power to become the sons of God, even to them that believe on his name*" (John 1:12).

In Revelation, the very last book of the Bible, we see God's final invitation: "*And the Spirit and the bride say, Come. And let him that heareth say, Come. And let him that is athirst come. And* ***whosoever will,*** *let him take the water of life freely*" (Revelation 22:17). As the old hymn says, "Whosoever will, may come." God wants everyone to be His child.

B. God will never disinherit a family member.

Once we have accepted God's gift of eternal life, we enter into a Father-child relationship with God. Many people wonder if this relationship can be broken by sin. Can someone who has genuinely accepted Christ as Saviour lose his salvation? The illustration of a parent-child relationship also helps us understand "eternal security."

First, the parent-child relationship is a **blood relationship**. Fellowship can be broken, but a blood relationship cannot be undone. A child can cease to get along with his parents, but nothing and no one can change that blood relationship. You will always be your parents' child, no matter how old you are, where you go, or what you do.

Accepting Christ as our Saviour places us in a blood relationship as well. Christ shed His blood for our sins on the Cross. The moment we receive Christ and become God's children, that blood covers our sins before God.

1 Peter 1:18–19

18 Forasmuch as ye know that ye were not redeemed with corruptible things, as silver and gold, from your vain conversation received by tradition from your fathers;
19 But with the precious blood of Christ, as of a lamb without blemish and without spot:

So we have a blood relationship with God, through Jesus Christ His Son. Our *fellowship* with God can be broken by sin, but our *relationship* with God can never be broken.

Another reason we know that this Father-child relationship can never be broken is that we were **born into the family** when we were "born again." A child can never become "unborn;" neither can we undo our spiritual birth.

Those who feel that sin could cause them to lose their relationship as a child of God should remember how they became a child of God.

EPHESIANS 2:8–9
8 For by grace are ye saved through faith; and that not of
yourselves: it is the gift of God:
9 Not of works, lest any man should boast.

To put it very simply: we did not get saved by being good, and we cannot stay saved by being good. The Galatians questioned Paul with this issue, and he answered them very emphatically: *"O foolish Galatians, who hath bewitched you, that ye should not obey the truth, before whose eyes Jesus Christ hath been evidently set forth, crucified among you? This only would I learn of you, Received ye the Spirit by the works of the law, or by the hearing of faith? Are ye so foolish? having begun in the Spirit, are ye now made perfect by the flesh?"* (Galatians 3:1–3).

No one can take your status as a child of your parents away from you, and no one can take your salvation and your status as a child of God away from you either.

JOHN 10:27–29
27 My sheep hear my voice, and I know them, and they
follow me:
28 And I give unto them eternal life; and they shall
never perish, ***neither shall any man pluck them out of***
my hand.

29 *My Father, which gave them me, is greater than all; and* ***no man is able to pluck them out of my Father's hand.***

What *does* happen when a child of God commits sin? We all know that, even as children of God, we will continue to do things that displease God.

1 John 1:8, 10

8 *If we say that we have no sin, we deceive ourselves, and the truth is not in us.*
10 *If we say that we have not sinned, we make him a liar, and his word is not in us.*

When a Christian sins, fellowship with God is broken because God will not tolerate sin. What happens next is very similar to what a wise parent does when his child disobeys. When your child displeases you, does he cease to be your child? No! You set appropriate consequences for his misbehavior—you punish the transgression. But you do not stop loving your child, and you do not stop being that child's parent.

Hebrews 12:6

6 *For whom the Lord loveth he chasteneth, and scourgeth every son whom he receiveth.*

To *chasten* means "to correct by punishment or reproof." To *scourge* is "to inflict severe suffering, vengeance, or punishment." [Source: *The American Heritage Dictionary of the English Language, Third Edition* Copyright ©1992 by Houghton Mifflin Company. Electronic version.] God will do whatever is necessary to correct our behavior, but He always corrects us with a view toward restoring us back into fellowship with Him. He disciplines us because He loves us.

II. Benefits of Being God's Child

Inherent in the hiring process of a company is the matter of "benefits." Insurance, paid holidays, paid vacation days, paid sick days, opportunity to contribute to a 401(k), and employee discounts are all things that may be included in a "benefits package."

PSALM 68:19
19 Blessed be the Lord, who daily loadeth us with benefits, even the God of our salvation. Selah.

The child of God receives an incredible "benefits package!"

A. Family name

When a child is born, he takes the special first name that is given to him, and he takes the last name of his family. His last name identifies him, and he carries it with him.

Illustration

Children with older brothers and sisters often learn the weight of a family name on their first day of school. Teachers easily form an impression of a child, even before getting to know him, based on the impression an older sibling left with them. Sometimes this is helpful, and sometimes it is not so helpful.

As children of God, we carry the name "Christians." Where did this name come from, and what does it mean? In Acts 11:26, the Bible says that *"the disciples were called Christians first in Antioch."* The name *Christian* means "a follower of Christ." The Bible does not say specifically who gave them this name or why. Many believe that the name "Christian" was intended to be a mockery at first; but, regardless of its origin, it certainly became a name that the disciples of Christ were proud to bear—a name that distinctly marked them as having been with Jesus.

Acts 4:13

13 *Now when they saw the boldness of Peter and John, and perceived that they were unlearned and ignorant men, they marvelled; and they took knowledge of them, that they had been with Jesus.*

Do you remember that the face of Moses was glowing when he came down from the mountain after having spent forty days alone with God (Exodus 34:29–35)? There is, or ought to be, something special about the people of God that is noticeable and noteworthy to those who do not know God. Can others look at us and say, "They are followers of Christ"?

B. Inheritance

As children of God, we have a family name of which we should be proud, and also, we have an inheritance. Paul mentions our inheritance as children of God several times:

Ephesians 1:11–18

11 *In whom also we have obtained an* ***inheritance****, being predestinated according to the purpose of him who worketh all things after the counsel of his own will:*
12 *That we should be to the praise of his glory, who first trusted in Christ.*
13 *In whom ye also trusted, after that ye heard the word of truth, the gospel of your salvation: in whom also after that ye believed, ye were sealed with that holy Spirit of promise,*

14 *Which is the earnest of our* ***inheritance*** *until the*
redemption of the purchased possession, unto the praise of
his glory.
15 *Wherefore I also, after I heard of your faith in the Lord*
Jesus, and love unto all the saints,
16 *Cease not to give thanks for you, making mention of*
you in my prayers;
17 *That the God of our Lord Jesus Christ, the Father of*
glory, may give unto you the spirit of wisdom and revelation
in the knowledge of him:
18 *The eyes of your understanding being enlightened;*
that ye may know what is the hope of his calling, and what
the riches of the glory of his ***inheritance*** *in the saints,*

Romans 8:16–18

16 *The Spirit itself beareth witness with our spirit, that*
we are the children of God:
17 ***And if children, then heirs; heirs of God, and joint-***
heirs with Christ; *if so be that we suffer with him, that we*
may be also glorified together.
18 *For I reckon that the sufferings of this present time are*
not worthy to be compared with the glory which shall be
revealed in us.

So, as children of God, we are heirs, and we have an inheritance—something from God that will in the future be ours. What is this inheritance? We can't describe it fully because "*Eye hath not seen, nor ear heard, neither have entered into the heart of man, the things which God hath prepared for them that love him*" (1 Corinthians 2:9). Here are some things we can say about this future state of the child of God:

1 Peter 1:4

4 *To an inheritance incorruptible, and undefiled, and that fadeth not away, reserved in heaven for you,*

Our inheritance is **incorruptible**—it cannot decay or deteriorate. It is imperishable. Unlike everything on earth which decays, our inheritance is perfect and will stay perfect.

Our inheritance is **undefiled**—unsoiled, perfectly clean, uncontaminated, unspotted, untainted. On this earth there is no such thing as "perfectly clean"; there is only an acceptable level of contamination, but our inheritance is undefiled.

Our inheritance **does not fade** away—it never changes; it never grows old; it never loses its freshness.

Our inheritance is **reserved in heaven** for us. We can rest assured that God is taking good care of the things that He has for us in the future. We can also rest assured that, no matter what we imagine beforehand, the reality will be even better!

C. Home

As the average American lifespan is lengthening (now between 75 and 80 years), we are seeing a growing need for assisted-living and long-term care facilities. Ideally, children should care for their parents themselves; although realistically, this is not always possible.

Let's read what Jesus said about God's long-term care facility for His children:

John 14:2–3

2 *In my Father's house are many mansions: if it were not so, I would have told you. I go to prepare a place for you.*

3 *And if I go and prepare a place for you, I will come again, and receive you unto myself; that where I am, there ye may be also.*

Jesus has been preparing this long-term care facility for us for a long time now, and He's waiting there to welcome us when our time comes.

The Thessalonians had questions, as many people do, about loved ones who had died. Paul gave them this wonderful assurance:

1 THESSALONIANS 4:13–18
13 *But I would not have you to be ignorant, brethren, concerning them which are asleep, that ye sorrow not, even as others which have no hope.*
14 *For if we believe that Jesus died and rose again, even so them also which sleep in Jesus will God bring with him.*
15 *For this we say unto you by the word of the Lord, that we which are alive and remain unto the coming of the Lord shall not prevent them which are asleep.*
16 *For the Lord himself shall descend from heaven with a shout, with the voice of the archangel, and with the trump of God: and the dead in Christ shall rise first:*
17 *Then we which are alive and remain shall be caught up together with them in the clouds, to meet the Lord in the air: and so shall we ever be with the Lord.*
18 *Wherefore comfort one another with these words.*

One day soon, Jesus will return for us in what we call the Rapture. Those Christians who have already died will rise first, and the rest of us will meet Him in the air. When we finally reach Heaven, we'll truly be Home!

D. Protection

God takes good care of His children, and we are assured of His protection. Nothing can happen to us without His permission.

Illustrations

God has given many examples of His watch care over His children:

God's Servant, Job

There came a point in Job's life when it seemed that his life was a complete mix of tragedies. Satan challenged God to lift His protection from Job; he accused Job of disloyalty and said that, without God's blessings, Job would curse God. God allowed Satan to take away Job's servants, his flocks, his herds, and even his own children (Job 1:13–19), but God refused to allow Satan to touch Job himself. Later on, God allowed Satan to take Job's health, but He refused to allow him to take his life.

Through Job's life we learn the greatness of God's protection—even Satan can only go as far against God's children as God will allow. God protects His children.

The Israelites at the Red Sea

In Exodus 14, the Israelites are encamped at the shore of the Red Sea. Through ten plagues, God had delivered His children from Egypt. Shortly after their release, Pharaoh changed his mind and began pursuing them with his armies.

With the Red Sea in front of them, the mountains to the side, and the Egyptian army behind, God's people were trapped. You can imagine the panic they must have felt, but Moses told them, *"Fear ye not, stand still, and see the salvation of the Lord, which he will shew to you to day...The* LORD *shall fight for you, and ye shall hold your peace*" (verses 13–14).

God took the pillar of cloud He had used to lead the Israelites and placed it between the Israelites and the Egyptian army. Behind that screen, God parted the waters of the Red Sea. The Israelites began to cross on the dry ground. As soon as the Egyptians could see what was happening, they chased after the Israelites. With the Israelites safely on the far shore, God released the waters and drowned the whole Egyptian army. God protected His children.

The Jews under King Ahasuerus

The book of Esther is the only book in the Bible that does not contain the word *God.* Yet, God's hand of protection is so evident in the ten-chapter story of deliverance. God arranged events so that a young Jewish lady, Esther, would be the queen of Persia at the same time wicked Haman plotted to exterminate the Jews. God gave Esther the courage to reveal Haman's plot to the king and intercede for the lives of her people. Once again, God protected His children.

The Prophet Elisha

In 2 Kings 6, the king of Israel sent an army to capture Elisha. The army located the city where Elisha was at the time and surrounded it. "*...And his servant said unto him, Alas, my master! how shall we do? And he answered, Fear not: for they that be with us are more than they that be with them. And Elisha prayed, and said,* LORD, *I pray thee, open his eyes, that he may see. And the* LORD *opened the eyes of the young man; and he saw: and, behold, the mountain was full of horses and chariots of fire round about Elisha*" (2 Kings 6:15–17).

God's protection surrounds us, and most of the time we don't even realize it. Even today, we see the protecting hand of God on Israel as it is surrounded by hostile neighbors. God continues to protect His children.

Nothing can separate us from the love of God (Romans 8:31–39), and God surely protects what He loves.

III. Being the Right Kind of Child

With the security of knowing we will always be God's child comes an increased desire to please our loving Heavenly Father. As a Father, God desires our growth in our relationship with Him. In what areas specifically can we please Him?

A. Obedience

The fifth commandment is, "*Honour thy father and thy mother: that thy days may be long upon the land which the Lord thy God giveth thee*" (Exodus 20:12).

A young child does not understand much, but he can (and should) be taught to obey. Parents who early on teach their children to obey will save both themselves and their children much trouble later. Proverbs contains many admonitions to teach children early.

Proverbs 22:15

15 *Foolishness is bound in the heart of a child; but the rod of correction shall drive it far from him.*

Proverbs 22:6

6 *Train up a child in the way he should go: and when he is old, he will not depart from it.*

Paul instructed children to simply obey their parents.

EPHESIANS 6:1
1 *Children, obey your parents in the Lord: for this is right.*

COLOSSIANS 3:20
20 *Children, obey your parents in all things: for this is well pleasing unto the Lord.*

Jeremiah 7:23 reveals a particular theme that God continually brings before His children: "...*Obey my voice, and I will be your God, and ye shall be my people: and walk ye in all the ways that I have commanded you, that it may be well unto you.*" God wants us to obey Him for *our* own good.

TEACHING TIP

Share a personal illustration of a time when you disobeyed your parents, thinking you knew what was best, but later found that your parents' instructions really were for your own good.

Surely, amidst the many stories we may have of times where we disobeyed, we also had at least some times of complete obedience. When we obeyed our parents, sooner or later, we were glad we did. We can rest assured that, when we obey God, we will be very glad we did!

Sadly many people don't obey their Heavenly Father by living according to His Word. James cautions us against living this way: "*But be ye doers of the word, and not hearers only, deceiving your own selves*" (James 1:22). Don't just *hear* the Word of God—*obey* the Word of

God (Ezra 7:10; James 4:17; Luke 6:46–49, 11:28, 12:47–48; John 13:17; Romans 2:13; 1 John 2:3).

As someone once said, "It's not how much Bible you *learn*, it's how much Bible you *live*." You and I may be a sad sermon illustration some day if we do not simply live by what we know.

"Knowledge without obedience only increases condemnation." [Source: *Pulpit Commentary*] In other words, we are responsible for what we know. We have the truth. We read it in God's Word, and we hear it preached and taught at church. We have no excuse, then, for failing to live by the truth.

As we've mentioned before, hearing the Word of God and not obeying it is like a man looking at himself in the mirror, seeing what needs to be done, but turning his back and walking away without making any changes (James 1:23–24). In contrast to the man who turns his back on the truth, the very next verse says, "*But whoso looketh into the perfect law of liberty, and continueth therein, he being not a forgetful hearer, but a doer of the work, this man shall be blessed in his deed.*" The blessed man is the one who hears the Word of God and *lives by it.*

When we consider the blessings God has promised for obedience and the consequences He has promised for disobedience, joyfully obeying our loving Heavenly Father is the only desirable option!

B. Faithfulness

As God's children, we owe Him our faithfulness and our devotion. God is an ever-faithful Father to us. "*If we believe not, yet he abideth faithful: he cannot deny himself*" (2 Timothy 2:13).

Twice in 1 Corinthians, Paul reminded us that *"God is faithful"* (1 Corinthians 1:9, 10:13).

Illustration

The motto of the U.S. Marine Corps, "semper fidelis," perfectly captures God's faithfulness to us. As Christians, we should strive to live by that motto as well: "Always Faithful—to our Heavenly Father."

Conclusion

Somewhere in the salutation of nearly all of Paul's epistles he mentions *"God our Father."* No matter what may have been the main subject of the letter, Paul wanted the believers to know first of all that God was their Father. Living in the light of that close relationship with the Lord allows everything else to fall into place. We must strive to be the right kind of children in order to be the fulfilled Christians God wants us to be.

Study Questions

1. How do we become a child of God?
   We are "born again." 1) Realize we are sinners and are condemned before God. 2) Know that Christ died for our sins. 3) Trust Christ for salvation.

2. Who is included in this invitation for salvation?
   Everyone is given an invitation to be saved. John 3:16, Romans 10:13, etc. "Whosoever will, may come."

3. What four benefits are we given as children of God?
   We are given a family name, an inheritance, a Home, and God's protection.

4. What two responsibilities should we fill to be the right kind of child?
   We must be obedient and faithful.

5. When did you become a Christian? Briefly describe your salvation testimony including the events that may have led to your salvation and what prompted you to choose to trust Christ as your Saviour.
   Answers will vary.

6. A benefit and responsibility of being a child of God is carrying the name "Christian." Are there any ways that you have dishonored the Father's reputation? If so, how can you make it right?
   Answers will vary.

7. How does eternal security tie in to God's promise of a home in Heaven? What verses support your answer?
Eternal security is the fulfillment of God's promise of a home in Heaven. It cannot be taken away or lost, no matter what you do. Galatians 3:1–3; John 10:27–29; Ephesians 2:8–9.

8. Describe the difference between being a *hearer* of the Word and a *doer* of the Word. What can you do to be a *doer* of the truths you've learned today?
A hearer of the Word listens without obeying, but a doer of the Word obeys the truths he hears. Answers will vary on the second part of this question.

Memory Verse

EPHESIANS 5:1–2

1 *Be ye therefore followers of God, as dear children.*
2 *And walk in love, as Christ also hath loved us, and hath given himself for us an offering and a sacrifice to God for a sweetsmelling savour.*

LESSON THIRTEEN

An Ambassador for Christ

Text

2 Corinthians 5:20

20 Now then we are ambassadors for Christ, as though God did beseech you by us: we pray you in Christ's stead, be ye reconciled to God.

Overview

An ambassador represents his leader in a foreign land. Christ has given us the privilege of representing Him here on this earth. He has given us privileged access to Him, a powerful defense against attacks of our adversary, and the ability to accomplish our assignment.

Lesson Theme

Our assignment as the Lord's ambassador is to go and preach the Gospel to all nations. Our time is limited, so with all haste we must fulfill the one assignment to which we are called.

Lesson Objectives

At the conclusion of the lesson, each student should:

1. Utilize the privileged access with God we possess as an ambassador of Christ.
2. Determine not to conform to this world, but rather maintain our distinction as followers of Christ.

3. Participate in carrying the Gospel to all parts of the earth.

Teaching Outline

Introduction

- I. The Ambassador's Access
  - A. Authorized access
  - B. Available access
- II. The Ambassador's Adversary
  - A. The adversary's attack
  - B. The ambassador's defense
- III. The Ambassador's Assignment
  - A. Go therefore
  - B. Go preach
- IV. The Ambassador's Address
  - A. His temporary address is earth.
  - B. His permanent address is Heaven.

Conclusion

LESSON THIRTEEN

An Ambassador for Christ

Text

2 CORINTHIANS 5:20

20 Now then we are ambassadors for Christ, as though God did beseech you by us: we pray you in Christ's stead, be ye reconciled to God.

Introduction

An ambassador represents his leader in a foreign land. Christ has given us the privilege of representing Him here on this earth. He has given us privileged access to Him, a powerful defense against attacks of our adversary, and the ability to accomplish our assignment.

I. The Ambassador's Access

By representing his leader and his country, an ambassador has privileges that most people do not.

> A diplomat's privileges are based on the principle of extraterritoriality. This principle, used in international law, includes the guarantee that people living in foreign countries remain under the authority of their own governments. Four important diplomatic privileges and immunities are:
>
> 1. Diplomats cannot be arrested for any reason. Their families usually share this exemption.
> 2. Their residences, papers, and effects cannot be searched or seized.
> 3. Their personal belongings cannot be taxed by the country in which they serve.
> 4. Diplomats, their families, and their staffs enjoy complete freedom of worship.
>
> ("Diplomacy," World Book 2001, CD-ROM edition)

A. Authorized access

The ambassador has high priority access to information and people because he is authorized. He has been specially chosen and appointed by the leader of the country to take on that responsibility. In the United States, the President appoints all ambassadors. They then must be approved by the Senate. Once an ambassador has been appointed and approved, he has the authority to represent the United States in a foreign country.

This concept so accurately applies to us as God's ambassadors. We have been chosen and appointed by our Leader to represent Him here.

John 20:21

21 *...Peace be unto you: as my Father hath sent me, even so send I you.*

John 15:16

16 *Ye have not chosen me, but I have chosen you, and ordained you, that ye should go and bring forth fruit, and that your fruit should remain: that whatsoever ye shall ask of the Father in my name, he may give it you.*

An official ambassador can convey special messages from the leader he represents. He sometimes carries a diplomatic pouch with a special seal. The ambassador protects that message and is faithful to deliver it.

As authorized representatives of the Lord Jesus Christ, we are commissioned to carry His message to the people of this world. The Apostle Paul spoke of "*the glorious gospel of the blessed God, which was committed to my trust*" (1 Timothy 1:11). Three times, Paul spoke of the Gospel as "***my** gospel*" (Romans 2:16, 16:25; 2 Timothy 2:8). He was committed to the message of God in a very personal way and shared that message with all who crossed his path.

B. Available access

An ambassador also has privileged access to his leader—his own king or president. At almost any time, the ambassador can request a meeting with his leader and receive high priority. The leader may summon the ambassador for a special meeting, and the ambassador will drop everything and travel back home to keep that appointment. Of course, today we have many ways of communicating that did not exist just a few years ago, but sometimes there is just no substitute for a face-to-face meeting. The ambassador and the leader are always available to speak to each other.

It is a blessed truth that we always have access to our King as well. We never have to set up an appointment or wait in line. We never get a busy signal, and we never have to leave a voicemail. We never have to play "phone tag." Christ is always available for us, and He gives us the wonderful privilege to "*pray without ceasing*" (1 Thessalonians 5:17).

Hebrews 4:15–16

15 *For we have not an high priest which cannot be touched with the feeling of our infirmities; but was in all points tempted like as we are, yet without sin.*

16 *Let us therefore* ***come boldly unto the throne of grace,*** *that we may obtain mercy, and find grace to help in time of need.*

We have constant access to the throne of grace. The Lord has authorized us for His work, and He is always available to give us what we need to carry out His mission.

Illustration

Christian martyrs who faced horrible persecution for the Lord could never have remained faithful without this access to their King for grace and strength. What if each of these men had not had ready access to his King?

- The Apostle Paul in the Mamertine prison, awaiting execution
- William Tyndale imprisoned in the castle of Vilvoorde (outside Brussels), awaiting execution for translating the Bible into English and preaching salvation by faith alone

- John Bunyan in Bedford prison for preaching the Gospel without a license

Even prison bars could not block their access to their King. God was just as available to them in their confinement as He was in the days when they served Him freely. No matter how dark the hour, no matter where we are, we can always come to our King.

Privileged access to the leader requires diligent communication. Some ambassadors fail in their mission because they don't maintain communication with their leader. We may fail in other things, but we must not fail to stay in close touch with our Lord.

II. The Ambassador's Adversary

It's not always easy to live in a foreign country for an extended length of time. Adversities in the form of struggles come, such as learning the language or adapting to the food and culture. An ambassador has to be able to adjust to all of these, while still maintaining his loyalty to and his identification with his native country.

In hostile countries, the ambassador has determined adversaries—people who are antagonistic to his mission. He may even live under a real possibility of assassination.

As ambassadors for Christ, we have a powerful adversary as well.

A. *The adversary's attack*

1 Peter 5:8

8 Be sober, be vigilant; because your adversary the devil, as a roaring lion, walketh about, seeking whom he may devour.

Illustration

In 1898, when East Africa was an English colony, British engineers and gangs of natives were building a railroad line. Two lions began preying on the workmen, and it seemed as though nothing could stop them. In spite of every precaution, nearly every night for several months the lions would carry off at least one native. Those lions brought the work to a complete halt for several weeks. You can imagine the terror of the natives. They were sure that the lions were devils appearing in lion bodies.

Finally, a man named Colonel J.H. Patterson was put in charge of the railroad project, and eventually he was able to kill both of the lions. He tells his story in the book *The Man-Eaters of Tsavo and Other East African Adventures.* Today these very lions are on display at the Field Museum of Natural History in Chicago.

The devil is compared to a roaring lion, a man-eater, looking for his prey, and he wants to devour us. If we belong to Christ, he can't get our souls—but he can seek to ruin our lives and our effectiveness for the Lord.

One of the adversary's greatest goals is for us to conform to this world. By blending in with the world, we lose the distinction maintained by a true follower of Christ.

An ambassador must make it clear that he is not a permanent resident in the country where he is serving. Some ambassadors stay too long in their field and become de-nationalized; they forget their first duty—to represent their own country and its leader.

Our first duty as an ambassador of Christ is to seek the lost and communicate Christ's offer of salvation to them. We must stay on task and not get distracted from our purpose.

1 John 2:15–16

15 *Love not the world, neither the things that are in the world. If any man love the world, the love of the Father is not in him.*

16 *For all that is in the world, the lust of the flesh, and the lust of the eyes, and the pride of life, is not of the Father, but is of the world.*

Our adversary, the devil, wants us to love the world and to become like the world, but we can only represent the Father and accurately display His holiness and love if we are separated from the world's lifestyle.

B. The ambassador's defense

Can we fight so powerful an enemy as Satan? What is our defense against conforming to this world? How can we maintain a holy life for the Lord?

Romans 12:1–2

1 *I beseech you therefore, brethren, by the mercies of God, that ye present your bodies a living sacrifice, holy, acceptable unto God, which is your reasonable service.*

2 *And be not conformed to this world: but be ye transformed by the renewing of your mind, that ye may prove what is that good, and acceptable, and perfect, will of God.*

Presenting our bodies as a living sacrifice means surrendering our wills to His will. We give up the ownership and the directorship of our lives to Him. This is "*our reasonable service.*" Those who would say, "It's my body, and I'll choose what to do with it" are being unreasonable. Ambassadors fulfill their leader's desires—that is the essence of their responsibility.

Transforming and renewing our minds is the next step. We can accomplish this by filling our minds with God's Word and shunning things which take our minds and hearts away from Him.

2 Corinthians 10:5
5 *Casting down imaginations, and every high thing that exalteth itself against the knowledge of God, and bringing into captivity every thought to the obedience of Christ.*

Proverbs 4:23
23 *Keep thy heart with all diligence; for out of it are the issues of life.*

We have a powerful adversary, but we have a mightier King! Submit to God's will for your life, and embrace His Word to renew your mind.

III. The Ambassador's Assignment

Our duty is to represent God here in this world, but our mission is to fulfill the Great Commission.

Matthew 28:18–20
18 *And Jesus came and spake unto them, saying, All power is given unto me in heaven and in earth.*
19 *Go ye therefore, and teach all nations, baptizing them in the name of the Father, and of the Son, and of the Holy Ghost:*
20 *Teaching them to observe all things whatsoever I have commanded you: and, lo, I am with you alway, even unto the end of the world. Amen.*

A. *Go therefore*

Notice the word *therefore* in Matthew 28:19. *Why* did Christ instruct us to go into all the world with the Gospel? Because He has all power (verse 18), and He promises to personally accompany us (verse 20). Again, we see that we are authorized by the Lord to fulfill our mission—Go!

We are commanded to go to all nations.

Some may be called to go personally to foreign lands (missionaries).

Others may be called to go to various places in their own home country (pastors, assistants, church planters, evangelists, Christian schoolteachers).

Some are called to stay right where they are and be faithful soulwinners there.

Every Christian needs to participate in some way. We can go, we can give, we can pray. We all have a part.

Proverbs 25:13

13 *As the cold of snow in the time of harvest, so is a faithful messenger to them that send him: for he refresheth the soul of his masters.*

Our responsibility to carry the message on behalf of our Leader requires faithfulness. Can God trust us to carry His message faithfully?

B. *Go preach*

In Mark 16:15 Jesus told us the message He wants us to carry when we go: "*Go ye into all the world, and preach the gospel to every creature*" (Mark 16:15). It's no use going if we are not carrying the message of the Gospel!

Paul carefully described the simple Gospel message.

1 Corinthians 15:1–4
1 *Moreover, brethren, I declare unto you the gospel*
which I preached unto you, which also ye have received,
and wherein ye stand;
2 *By which also ye are saved, if ye keep in memory what*
I preached unto you, unless ye have believed in vain.
3 *For I delivered unto you first of all that which I also*
received, how that ***Christ died for our sins*** *according to*
the scriptures;
4 *And that* ***he was buried****, and that* ***he rose again the***
third day *according to the scriptures:*

The Gospel carries tremendous power.

Romans 1:16
16 *For I am not ashamed of the gospel of Christ: for it is the power of God unto salvation to every one that believeth; to the Jew first, and also to the Greek.*

The duty of an ambassador for Christ could be summed as follows (compare to our key verse): "I am an ambassador for Christ—He sent me to beseech you to be reconciled to God." This is the message of the Gospel and the ministry of Christ's ambassadors.

2 Corinthians 5:18
18 *And all things are of God, who hath* ***reconciled*** *us to himself by Jesus Christ, and hath given to us the ministry of* ***reconciliation;***

To be reconciled means "to reestablish a close relationship between two parties." Man's fellowship with God was broken by sin. The Son of God came to earth to shed His blood and die for that sin. The price has been paid. Forgiveness has been purchased. The way of reconciliation is open, but man has to accept the gift of God. That is our message. Delivering this message, in personal one-on-one soulwinning, preaching behind a pulpit, or any other method of proclaiming the Gospel, is the assignment of every ambassador of Christ.

TEACHING TIP

This would be an excellent opportunity to encourage your students to take part in the outreach ministries of your church. Invite them to accompany you out on visitation or soulwinning. Briefly demonstrate how to give out a Gospel tract. Encourage them to constantly consider the spiritual condition of those around them.

IV. The Ambassador's Address

Where does an ambassador officially live? Is his address located in his home country or in his country of residence? According to the dictionary, an ambassador is "A diplomatic official...representative in residence by one government or sovereign to another, *usually for a specific length of time.*" [Source: *The American Heritage Dictionary of the English Language*, Third Edition Copyright ©1992 by Houghton Mifflin Company. Electronic version.] An ambassador does not normally have his job for life. American ambassadors are appointed by the president, so the agreement may be that the ambassador will only serve as long as that president holds office. A new president may want to choose a new ambassador. Or perhaps, the ambassador may only agree to a certain term of service for his own personal reasons. The point is this: the ambassador's real home is his native country, and his stay in the foreign country is only temporary.

A. His temporary address is earth.

We are placed here on this earth temporarily to serve as ambassadors for Christ. We have a mission, a specific job to accomplish, and this world is only a temporary place of residence for us—we are only here for a certain length of time. Some lengths are shorter than others, but nobody stays forever. There will come a time when God will call His ambassadors out of their assignments and back to the home country. One song says, "This world is not my home; I'm just a-passing through…."

Meanwhile, Christ desires our earthly homes to serve as embassies of Heaven. For example, God designed the marriage relationship to be a picture of Christ's relationship with the church. The wife is to picture the submission we give to Christ, and the husband is to picture the love Christ gives to us.

EPHESIANS 5:22–25

22 *Wives, submit yourselves unto your own husbands, as unto the Lord.*
23 *For the husband is the head of the wife, even as Christ is the head of the church: and he is the saviour of the body.*
24 *Therefore as the church is subject unto Christ, so let the wives be to their own husbands in every thing.*
25 *Husbands, love your wives, even as Christ also loved the church, and gave himself for it;*

Is your home an embassy of Heaven? A home is not a Christian home simply because Christians live in it. A Christian home is established when Christians follow God's principles and serve Him together.

B. His permanent address is Heaven.

Jesus made it very clear that we are to look to Heaven as our real home:

MATTHEW 6:19–21
19 *Lay not up for yourselves treasures upon earth, where moth and rust doth corrupt, and where thieves break through and steal:*
20 *But lay up for yourselves treasures in heaven, where neither moth nor rust doth corrupt, and where thieves do not break through nor steal:*
21 *For where your treasure is, there will your heart be also.*

Paul also encouraged us to look ahead to our real Home:

2 CORINTHIANS 4:17–5:2
17 *For our light affliction, which is but for a moment, worketh for us a far more exceeding and eternal weight of glory;*
18 *While we look not at the things which are seen, but at the things which are not seen: for the things which are seen are temporal; but the things which are not seen are eternal.*
1 *For we know that if our earthly house of this tabernacle were dissolved, we have a building of God, an house not made with hands, eternal in the heavens.*
2 *For in this we groan, earnestly desiring to be clothed upon with our house which is from heaven:*

The song "What a Day that Will Be" reminds us of the joys of our eternal Home.

> There is coming a day when no heartaches shall come
> No more clouds in the sky, no more tears to dim the eye.

All is peace forevermore, on that happy golden shore
What a day, glorious day that will be.

What a day that will be, when my Jesus I shall see,
And I look upon His face, the one who saved me by His grace.
When He takes me by the hand, and leads me through the Promised Land
What a day, glorious day that will be.

There'll be no sorrow there, no more burdens to bear
No more sickness, no pain, no more parting over there.
And forever I will be with the one who died for me
What a day, glorious day that will be.
—Jim Hill

Illustration

The story is told of a missionary couple who spent over fifty years in their field of service. Unable to continue their ministry because of poor health, they boarded a ship to return to America. As the ship neared the harbor in New York, they were touched to see a tremendous crowd waiting for them. Welcome banners billowed in the wind, and bands sounded out a heartening greeting.

As the ship approached the dock, the missionary couple strained to see the faces of their loved ones and prayer warriors. It was then that they realized that the crowd, the banners, the bands were not for them. Apparently, there was a political celebrity on their ship as well, and the welcome was for him.

Disembarking, the missionaries sadly realized that there was *no one* there to greet them, to thank them for their service, or to welcome them home. But the wife took her husband's arm and whispered, "Honey, we're not home yet."

Our home country is not wherever we live and serve on earth—it is Heaven. As ambassadors for Christ, may we remember that our rewards are above, and may we faithfully serve our King.

Conclusion

One day soon, our King will call us home. We all long to hear Him say, "Well done, thou good and faithful servant." Are we representing Him well? Are we being faithful ambassadors?

Study Questions

1. What special message are we as ambassadors commissioned to carry?
   We are commissioned to carry the Gospel.

2. What responsibility does privileged access to the leader require?
   Privileged access to the leader requires diligent communication.

3. Who is our adversary in this world? What is one of his greatest goals for us studied in this lesson?
   The devil is our adversary. His goal is for us to conform to this world.

4. What verses explain our greatest defense against this adversary?
   Romans 12:1–2: "I beseech you therefore, brethren, by the mercies of God, that ye ***present your bodies a living sacrifice****, holy, acceptable unto God, which is your reasonable service. And be not conformed to this world: but* ***be ye transformed by the renewing of your mind,*** *that ye may prove what is that good, and acceptable, and perfect, will of God."*

5. What steps are you taking to ensure your fulfillment of the Great Commission?
   Answers will vary but may include carrying tracts, personal soulwinning, giving to missions.

6. Since this home on earth is only temporary, what are you doing to ensure your home remains an embassy of Heaven?
   Answers will vary but may include family devotions, personal accountability to a spouse, going to church as a family.

7. Besides giving God His tithe, share a recent experience where you have deliberately laid up treasure in Heaven.
   Answers will vary.

8. What do you most look forward to about your eternal home?
   Answers will vary.

Memory Verse

2 Corinthians 5:20

20 Now then we are ambassadors for Christ, as though God did beseech you by us: we pray you in Christ's stead, be ye reconciled to God.

For additional Christian growth resources visit **www.strivingtogether.com**